Talkin' Trash

Basketball's
Greatest Insults

Kevin Nelson

A Fireside Book Published by Simon & Schuster
New York London Toronto Sydney Tokyo Singapore

F

FIRESIDE
Simon & Schuster Building
Rockefeller Center
1230 Avenue of the Americas
New York, New York, 10020

Designed by Bonni Leon
Manufactured in the United States of America

1   3   5   7   9   10   8   6   4   2

Library of Congress Cataloging in Publication Data
Nelson, Kevin, date.
Talkin' trash: basketball's greatest insults / Kevin Nelson.
p.   cm.
"A Fireside Book."
Includes index.
1. Basketball—Quotations, maxims, etc. 2. Invective. I. Title.
GV885.N33 1993
796.323—dc20   93-4342
                                          CIP
ISBN 0-671-76067-X

Acknowledgments

At the risk of sounding like Tommy Lasorda, who thanked everyone including the Great Dodger in the Sky in his book, I would like to express my gratitude not only to the people who contributed to *Talkin' Trash: Basketball's Greatest Insults,* but to all four insult volumes. They include, in no particular order: Mike Lupica, Jim Murray, Lowell Cohn, Cameron Stauth, John Hillyer, Lee Daniel Levine, Bruce Jenkins, Mike Littwin, Tony Kornheiser, Norman Chad, Steve Wulf, Steve Rushin, Jack McCallum, Steve Kelley, Joe Gosen, Brad Mangin, Kenneth Lee, Jan Hubbard, Tom Fitzgerald, Scott Ostler, John Feinstein, Steve Bitker, Steve Tady, Dan Shaughnessy, Allan Malamud, David Nelson, Jim Larson, Mark Heisler, Gene Wojciechowski, Harvey Araton, Filip Bondy, and many many others.

Contents

Preface

Anybody who plays or watches basketball knows that it's a verbal game. People are talking all the time: the players on the court, the coaches, and the spectators who encircle them. It's the same in pickup basketball as it is in the pros. The patter is part of it.

This is my fourth book of sports insults. First came *Baseball's Greatest Insults*, followed by a collection on football. Then, this year, two more published by Fireside: *Baseball's Even Greater Insults* and now *Talkin' Trash: Basketball's Greatest Insults*.

When I first started doing these books it was thought that of all the major sports, only baseball would have enough lore and material to fill an entire volume. Baseball insults have, in fact, filled two volumes so far, but what I've found along the way is that every sport—and basketball belongs at the top of the list in this regard—has a rich oral and written tradition in which the sharp one-liner, the cutting insult, the comedy roast joke, and even the ill-tempered diatribe all play prominent roles.

Why do people, especially sports fans, like insults? The fact that many of the insults are funny is an obvious part of it. Insults are often cruelly honest; they don't portray people in the way the public relations professionals want you to see them. Sometimes an insult will give you more insight into a person than anything else you'll ever read or hear about him. I think there's also a democratic aspect to an insult. These athletes are fabulously wealthy and famous, and insulting them is a way to bring them back to terra firma.

But I try not to analyze the appeal of these insults too much; all I do is collect them. And I hope that basketball fans—people who love the verbal rhythms and lively patter of basketball, the trash-talkin', in-your-face city game—will enjoy this collection as well.

—Kevin Nelson

The Good, the Bad, and the Bald: Michael Jordan and the Bad Boys of Detroit

There is no bigger star in all of sports than Michael Jordan. His good-guy image and gravity-defying acrobatics on a basketball court have made him a role model for youngsters all across the world. His opposite number in the NBA are the Bad Boys of the Detroit Pistons. They're basketball's version of the Dead End Kids, and as role models they're about as good as the guys on Death Row at San Quentin. Nevertheless, these two rivals have figured prominently in recent NBA history, so it seemed fitting to begin this collection with them.

Michael Jordan: Man . . . or God?

Michael Jordan is the greatest basketball player in the history of the universe. Very few people would dispute that. But some individuals, such as New York columnist Mike Lupica, are getting just a little bit sick and tired of hearing about it.

"The truth is, if I could be like Mike—or Michael, for that matter—I think I'd try to be a little more invisible," Lupica wrote after the Bulls' first championship in 1991. "Nike. Gatorade. McDonald's. Hanes. The Michael Jordan television special. "Saturday Night Live." That hype started to get a little tiresome last spring during the National Basketball Association finals. Good grief. Jordan wasn't just a great player trying to win his first pro championship. That wasn't big enough for NBC. Instead they had to make it a religious experience.

Michael Jordan, in a familiar pose, surrounded by microphones after a Chicago victory. (Photo by Brad Mangin)

"If Jordan didn't get the NBA title, there was no reason for any of us to go on," Lupica continues. "When the NBC cameras finally found him, kissing the trophy in the locker room after the Bulls had defeated the Lakers, we were presented with a bigger tearjerker than the parting scene in *ET.* Air Grail had finally won."

As Air Grail's fame and endorsement portfolio has become more and more celestial in nature, some earthbound souls have criticized him for being virtually invisible on social or political issues. "What has Michael Jordan ever said, other than how much money he makes?" scoffs Bill Walton, the former NBA and UCLA star now turned TV analyst. Tom Callahan, the *Washington Post* writer, agrees: "Beyond much doubt now, Jordan is the finest athlete and most tiresome person in the country."

Remarking on Michael's well-publicized golf and card gambling losses to some individuals of rather dubious reputation, Callahan says, "Away from the court, Jordan stands for gullibility. On the golf course, he is the unexpected heir to boxer Joe Louis, although the sucker's method of payment has been modernized. After every hole, Louis would dip his magnificent fist into a deep pants pocket and pull out a divot of crisscrossed dollar bills. Then he silently would offer it around for every smiling shark to take a little munch. In contrast, Jordan's ego bets are paid off by six-figure checks through his agency."

(Add Dick Schaap on Michael's gambling embarrassments: "The basketball season hasn't even begun, and already Michael Jordan has come up smelling like a rose—Pete Rose.")

On the issue of Michael's responsibilities to society at large or the black community in particular, it is worth noting that both Callahan and Walton are white. Nor does one find similar criticisms of Larry Bird or other white stars because they have not spoken out on the major issues of our time. Nevertheless, at least one black NBA player—indeed, a teammate on the Bulls—has criticized Jordan on this point as well. After the Los Angeles riots of 1992, Craig Hodges said that a celebrity and role model of the magnitude of Michael Jordan should not remain silent any longer.

"When they came to Michael after the LA deal went down and asked him what he thought, his reply was that he wasn't really up on what was going on. I can understand that, but at the same time, that's a bailout situation, because you are bailing out when some heat is coming on you. We can't bail anymore," said Hodges.

"Leadership in America is the athletes and entertainers. That's why I feel I have to start speaking out. On one hand, being in this league, you have a right to make as much as you can. But you have a responsibility. A lot of us don't look at the responsibility end of it as much as we do our right to ask for as much as we can get."

Further Comments on Michael's Golf Game

"The next guy that says, 'After the NBA, Michael is going to play the Tour' gets 10 whacks with a niblick. Jordan is about as close to making the Tour as Ian Woosnam is to dunking a basketball. . . . Head to head, Woosnam only beats Jordan by about 14 shots. To say that Jordan could learn in the off season what Woos-

nam has spent 12 hours a day perfecting since he was a kid is a flat-out insult."
—*Rick Reilly*, sportswriter

"I'll be playing center for the Bulls before he's on tour."
—golf pro *Peter Jacobsen*, asked if Michael Jordan had a future on the PGA tour

Michael Jordan Talks Candidly (For a Change)

The definitive book on Michael Jordan is *The Jordan Rules,* Sam Smith's behind-the-scenes look at the Bulls' 1990–91 championship season. A *Chicago Tribune* beat writer who's covered the team for many years, Smith revealed a side of Jordan that was somewhat different from his highly controlled "I Like Mike" public persona. Here are a few samples of the real Michael Jordan talking off-the-cuff about himself, his teammates, Bulls management, his peers in the NBA, and other subjects, as quoted in Smith's book.

Assessing the Bulls during the 1990 playoffs: "I looked over and saw Horace and Scottie screwing around, joking and messing up. They've got the talent, but they don't take it seriously. And the rookies were together, as usual. They've got no idea what it's all about. The white guys [John Paxon, Ed Nealy], they work hard but they don't have the talent. And the rest of them? Who knows what to expect? They're not good for much of anything."

On Bulls management (prior to the club's 1991 title): "They're not interested in winning. They just want to sell tickets, which they can do because of me."

On what he would do if he were coach of the Bulls: "I know what I would do if I were coaching. I'd determine our strengths and weaknesses and utilize them. And it's pretty clear what our strength is."

On what would happen if he became general manager: "If I were general manager, we'd be a better team."

On himself when he was a young player: "I thought of myself first, the team second. I always wanted my team to be successful. But I wanted to be the main cause."

After some Cleveland Cavalier players accused him of hotdogging and taking too many shots in a game: "I wouldn't be shooting so many times if I weren't open."

On Piston Bad Boy and rebounder extraordinaire Dennis Rodman: "He's a flopper. He just falls down and tries to get the calls. That's not good defense."

On Nets guard Reggie Theus: "I hate his game. He's so selfish, always berating the referees and yelling out there."

On former Bulls teammate Dennis Hopson: "You can see it in his eyes. He's scared. He's got no heart."

Jordan was always goofing on Bulls rookie Larry Sanders, whom Jordan accused of being lazy. "Hey," Jordan said after Sanders slammed one day in practice, "the No Doz must've worn off." Then, after hearing that Sanders signed a 10-day contract with Charlotte, Michael commented, "It's probably a 12-day. He needs two days to wake up."

To benchwarmer Charles Davis, as Davis was sorting through some Bulls tickets that he was going to give out to his family coming to the game that night: "They don't need a ticket to watch you sitting on the bench," said Michael. "They can go to your house for that."

On being on the floor with the Chicago reserves: "I hate being out there with those garbagemen. They don't get you the ball."

Michael Dishes Stacey

One of Jordan's favorite whipping boys on the Bulls is center Stacey King, a former number one draft pick from Oklahoma who's turned out to be nothing more than a left-handed Will Perdue. After seeing King walk into the locker room carrying a box, Jordan said: "I hope there's a jump shot in there." Then there was an all-out exchange between the two men during the 1990–91 season, in which Jordan launched off on King after a game, saying,

"You ever hear of a guy, 6'11", maybe 260 pounds, a guy big and fat like that and he can't get but two rebounds, if that many, running all over the damn court and he gets two rebounds." Jordan went on, "Big guy like that, and he gets one rebound. Can't even stick his ass into people and get more than that."

This drew an angry reaction from King. "Fuck you, Michael Jordan," he said. "All you're interested in is scoring and taking every shot. Maybe if you passed the ball to somebody else for a change instead of worrying about the scoring title, somebody else on this team could do something."

Undaunted, Mike kept right on teasing: "Big fat, fat guy. One rebound in three games. Power forward. Maybe they should call it powerless forward."

Michael, Jerry, and Toni

For many years Michael's biggest on-court feud was with the Bad Boys of Detroit, but off the court he did his sparring with his own general manager, Jerry Krause. Although two world championships have gone a long way toward healing their rift, Krause and Jordan did not get along because, in Jordan's view, the man in charge of assembling players for the Bulls was a screw-up. After Portland acquired Walter Davis during the 1991 season, Jordan saw it as a case of a rival trying to strengthen its lineup while his own team twiddled its thumbs. "It's the same old stuff with this organization," he said. "I'll tell you what: If I was the general manager, the Bulls would be a much stronger team." It got so bad at one point that Jordan and Krause stopped speaking to each other—"which is good," Michael commented. "That's all I ever wanted."

A real sore spot for Jordan—and Scottie Pippen, as well—was Krause's big bucks pursuit of Toni Kukoc, widely regarded as the best player in European basketball. The 6'10" Kukoc, says one sportswriter, "could be the best thing to come out of Europe since the miniskirt." Chicago owns his NBA rights, and Bulls general manager Jerry Krause reportedly offered him close to $4 million a year to get him to ply his talents in the U.S. of A. Jordan bitterly resented this, especially since the Bulls were offering more money to Kukoc than they were to Pippen, who was then renegotiating his contract. "That was a terrible thing," said Jordan. "I blame Jerry Krause for that." Jordan denigrated Kukoc's talents as a basketball player as well: "Wait until he gets an elbow in the face from Laimbeer. He won't be going to the basket again. I know he looks good, but that's against college players. He has no idea what the NBA is all about."

Irritated as hell at the Bulls management, Jordan and Pippen got a chance to dish Toni in person at the 1992 Olympic Games, when Kukoc's national team from Croatia played the Dream Team. The Americans smashed the Croats of course, and as the old joke goes, Pippen and Jordan covered Kukoc so tightly that when he went to the bathroom at halftime, Scottie handed him the tissue and Michael pulled the lever.

After the game—Kukoc's line read 0–0–0, or something close— Scottie Pippen jabbed the needle in just a little bit more. "Toni Kukoc could be a good player," he said, "but he's in the right league right now." Ouch.

Though Pippen was probably right, some people thought that the two Bulls should have shown more respect for international diplomacy. After all, it was Jerry Krause they were mad at, not Kukoc. "Toni Kukoc of Croatia was not ashamed," Mitch Albom wrote after the U.S. pasting of Croatia. "He knew he could play better. But for tonight, he was simply glad to face his heroes—even if few of them did any more than loosely shake his hand. Talking in that hallway, it was obvious there are at least two things Kukoc has more of than some of his NBA rivals: (1) The ability to speak another language, (2) Class."

The Jordannaires

Until they helped Chicago win a pair of world championships, the guys who played with Michael Jordan on the Bulls were known as "the Jordannaires"—or "my supporting cast," as Michael has called them. Basically, they passed Michael the ball and tried not to get in his way when he was scoring 40, 50 points in a game. Although their reputations have improved a little over the years (notably that of Scottie Pippen, now a star in his own right), they're still essentially a bunch of guys who are lucky as hell they happened to land on the same team as Michael Jordan.

Stacey King

"It's nice to see Stacey King has found a niche with the Bulls— taking vengeful cheap shots at opponents who rough up Michael

Jordan. It's the least an $8 million flop can do to make himself useful."
> —*John Hillyer*, sportswriter

"How can that piece of shit be making more money than me?"
> —*Scottie Pippen*, upon learning in 1990 that King's salary was bigger than his

"A two-year-old could get hit in the head with more rebounds than that."
> —Bulls assistant coach *John Bach*, after King got only one rebound in two full games

"He can't guard a safe when it's stationed more than five feet from the basket."
> —*Jack McCallum*, sportswriter

"Had a season that befits a man with the forename of a woman and the surname of a deskbound radio talk show host."
> —*Rotisserie League Basketball*

Bill Cartwright

"Mr. Bill appears to be in the throes of arthritis every time he launches his ugly shot."
> —*Tom Weir*, columnist

"He's so awkward that it's hard not to be injured when you're around him."
> —*Hakeem Olajuwon*, whose eye socket was fractured by a Cartwright elbow in a notorious 1991 incident (Olajuwon is one of many players over the years who've been injured by Cartwright's flailing, disjointed playing style)

"Any time you have a player with a history like Cartwright's, I think you have to take a close look when something like this happens. . . . We all know you can make something look unintentional even if it's intentional."

> —Houston GM *Steve Patterson*, irate over the Olajuwon elbowing

Craig Hodges

"He proved he can bury the three with the best by making 19 straight at the [1991] All Star Game's three-point shooting contest. Now if the NBA would just get rid of those defensive players."

> —*Rotisserie League Basketball*

Will Perdue

"He doesn't deserve to be named after a Big Ten school."

> —*Michael Jordan*, on his Bulls teammate (Jordan always referred to Perdue as "Will Vanderbilt," after the school he did come from)

"Perdue was said to be on the outs with Michael Jordan. Gee, we wonder who will win that power struggle."

> —*Rotisserie League Basketball*

"If Bill Cartwright plays until he's 50, Will Perdue will still be his backup."

> —Bulls assistant coach *John Bach*, having grown disillusioned over the one-time highly touted center's inability to do anything worthwhile on a basketball court

How the Bulls Assess Michael

Ah, but playing with Michael is a dream come true for these guys, right? Sometimes, sometimes not. Like everyone else, they are in awe of his talent. But there are times when they also wish he'd pass them the ball, too.

John Paxson, one of the Jordannaires, shares a word with Vlade Divac, a Yugoslavian member of the Showtime crowd. (Photo by Brad Mangin)

"Do you know who's the biggest obstacle to us running? Michael Jordan, that's who. He won't let go of the ball."
> —*Doug Collins*, former Bulls coach, on why Chicago wasn't running—or winning

"He's the greatest athlete I've ever seen. Maybe the greatest athlete ever to play any sport. He can do whatever he wants. It all comes so easy to him. He's just not a basketball player."
> —*Bill Cartwright*, during a low point in the team's 1990–1991 season

"It's hard playing on a team with Michael Jordan, because you're always the reason the team lost."
> —former Bull *Dave Corzine*, on Jordan's tendency to complain when his teammates screw up (though he's quieter when he screws up)

But Really, How Would the Bulls Shape Up Without Michael Jordan?

"When he's not in there, they're pretty much of a joke."
> —*Wayman Tisdale*, Sacramento Kings

"We're just as good as they are. Take Michael Jordan off that team and who the hell do they have? Who the hell do they have over there? Nobody."
> —*Reggie Miller*, Indiana Pacers

"Yo, scrubeenies, think about this the next time you're riding pine: You probably wouldn't be cashing as many playoff checks if you were getting more time on the floor."
> —*The Sporting News,* on complaints by some of Jordan's teammates that they weren't getting enough playing time

"Jordan must be a great player to win it with so many stiffs."
> —*Doug Moe*, opposing coach

Over the Years with the Bad Boys

Chicago versus Detroit. Michael versus Isiah and Rodman. The Jordannaires versus the Bad Boys. Bill Laimbeer versus Chicago Stadium. In the late eighties and early nineties, this was the best rivalry in basketball, the equal of the Lakers–Celtics struggles in the Magic and Bird era. Every good melodrama needs a villain, of course, and this role was played to the hilt by the fearsome Bad Boys of Detroit. Everybody outside the state of Michigan hated them and their body-slamming style of ball.

"If you laid Bill Laimbeer, Dennis Rodman, and the rest of the Detroit Pistons end to end in the Mojave Desert, it would be a good idea to leave them there."
—*Henry Schulman*, critic

"I'm not interested in them. Why should I give a shit about them? There is some obligation you have for kids, and to have a kid go around saying, 'I'll win and be famous, vicious, dirty and bad.' That's no image for kids."
—*Red Auerbach*

"Rod Thorn can kiss my ass. Thorn's biased. He's narrow-minded. I don't care what he thinks about me, 'cause I feel the same about him."
—Piston forward *Rick Mahorn*, after the NBA's director of operations fined him $5,000 for elbowing Mark Price, one of many such incidents in Mahorn's career

"What Mahorn did was more than an attempt to stop Mo from scoring. He grabbed him and threw him down."
—Hawks coach *Mike Fratello*, after a hard Rick Mahorn foul on Moses Malone

"The most bush league thing that's ever been done to me."
—*Kevin McHale*, after Mahorn stepped on McHale's broken foot—on purpose. The Celtics star then told Mahorn, "My foot will get better. But you'll still be 6'7" and fat, and I'm going to go at you."

"If we play the Pistons again in the playoffs, we'll need the three-knockdown rule."

> —*Charles Barkley*, after the infamous "Malice at the Palace" dust-up between Barkley's Sixers and the Bad Boys in the 1990 playoffs

"Well, that's one way to stop him, even if it isn't the cleanest of plays."

> —Phoenix coach *Cotton Fitzsimmons*, watching James Edwards grab Michael Jordan by the ankle and trip him up as Jordan tried to take off on a fast break

"When a hockey game breaks out in the NBA, two things are almost always certain: (1) Laimbeer or Rodman had a hand in it, and (2) one of them held his palms up and shrugged his shoulders before it was over."

> —*Inside Sports* magazine

"Sure, Laimbeer has the Academy Award flop on defense going for him, but Rodman has the peacock strut, the waving fists, the cocky, elbows-up trot *and* the Academy Award flop."

> —*Jack McCallum*, sportswriter

"Man, sometimes I just feel like killing that guy."

> —Eastern Conference coach on Rodman, as quoted by McCallum

"Horace Grant said he's going to remember for the rest of his life when we walked off the court, and we showed no class? Just forget about it. We never downgraded anyone when we won the championship."

> —*Dennis Rodman*, giving his version of the controversial episode in which the beaten Piston starters walked off the floor before the end of their game with the Chicago Bulls in the 1991 Eastern Conference championship finals

"I guess I don't have a lot of class, but I didn't see it last year either when the Pistons didn't shake the hands of the Chicago players."
>   —Utah coach *Jerry Sloan*, following a tiff with Rodman in a 1992 game in which the Pistons forward taunted Sloan and Sloan responded by blowing him a kiss and refusing to shake his hand

"In the meantime, Detroit's two-year Reign of Terror is history. Just what was Dennis Rodman doing shoving Scottie Pippen into the first row of seats after both he and Bill Laimbeer fouled the Bulls forward in the second quarter of game four? I mean, the foul was hard enough. It kept Pippen from an easy two and in and of itself, it was a relatively clean play. But Rodman's schoolyard shove of Pippen into the first row was as cheap a shot as I've seen in the NBA in years."
>   —sportswriter *Jeff Chapman*, following the Bulls' 1991 playoff win over Detroit and Rodman's blatant cheap shot on Pippen

"He could have hurt him. It was ridiculous."
>   —*Rod Thorn*, vice president of NBA operations, on why he was fining Rodman $5,000 for that play

"I don't think Rodman wrote it. I'm not convinced Rodman is intelligent enough to write a letter like that."
>   —*Scottie Pippen*, explaining why he would not accept Rodman's written apology for the incident

"Well, one look at our Cheap Shot Scoreboard shows the Pistons up 8–1. Rodman is having a fine half with five, and Laimbeer is running second with two. What do you think, Pat?"
>   —*Bob Costas*, during halftime of that game

"Well, every time Chicago has the ball, five Pistons are committing fouls. It's as if to say, 'Well, the officials can only call one at a time, so we get away with four.' You know, Michael Jordan said be-

fore the game: 'People want to push this kind of basketball out.'
The Bulls are 24 minutes away from doing just that."
—*Pat Riley*, in reply to Costas

And What About Chuck Daly, the Man Who Guided the Bad Boys to Their Two World Titles?

"He's not one of my favorite coaches. When they win, they've got
a lot of excuses. When they lose, they have a lot of excuses."
—*Karl Malone*, Utah Jazz forward, during the 1989–90
season

"Anyone who can take Bill Laimbeer and James Edwards—two
of the biggest defensive stiffs in the league—and make the defense
the best in the league is a brilliant man."
—Pistons front-office person, as quoted by *Newsday*

Chuck Explains How He Handled the Bad Boys and, Indeed, How He Manages the Modern Athlete

"You've got this kid and he makes $10 million—whatever. But
these guys are no different from the kids I coached at Punxsutawney
High School. Because you know what they're interested in? Points
scored, rebounds, minutes played. All the basic children's things.
It's a children's game, so that's kind of their mentality."

Cry Baby

The least popular and most childish of the now-defunct Bad
Boys is Bill Laimbeer, the tall whiny white guy in the middle. Here
are some more assessments of Big Bad Bill:

"I assume his parents like him. But you'd have to verify that."
—*Kurt Rambis*

"If the NHL needs a new goon, consider Bill Laimbeer of the Pistons. Maybe Laimbeer could go to Pittsburgh to protect Mario

Lemieux. Then he could see firsthand what it feels like to be on the receiving end of a chop, slash or check."
>   —fan, writing to *The Sporting News*

"It was intentional, and if the fine wasn't $7,000, I would have come over and punched him in the mouth. Somebody has got to do something about him."
>   —Indiana's *Vern Fleming*, after receiving a flagrant Laimbeer elbow in the mouth

"He fouled me, he tripped me, and he kicked me. A leopard doesn't change his spots. I was surprised at myself for reacting."
>   —the Bulls' *Horace Grant*, after a near-brawl with the Pistons center (following a collision, Laimbeer, lying on the court, had leg-whipped Grant as he was falling down)

"A 6'10" white guy who can't jump over a piece of paper."
>   —*Charles Barkley*, on Laimbeer

"The whiniest, the most despicable, the most disgusting guy in the league."
>   —more from *Barkley* on Laimbeer

"I would gladly chip in and pay part of his fines every time he smacks Bill Laimbeer."
>   —Utah Jazz GM *Frank Layden*, on Barkley's legendary battles with Laimbeer

"The premier why-ner, as in: "Why me? Wha'd I do?' Lam's repertoire of expressions after a foul is called on him ranges from the glassy Ivan Drago glare to the infantile I'm-gonna-hold-my-breath-until-you-change-that-call pose."
>   —sportswriter *Jeff Weinstock*, nominating Laimbeer to his "All-Whiner" team

"Talk about nightmares in the daytime: Can you imagine Bill Laimbeer in that plastic mask on a Wheaties box?"
—*Inside Sports* magazine

Laimbeer has said that after his retirement, he'd like to take some of his Piston teammates back into the woods with him for some hunting and fishing. Sportswriter Mitch Albom imagines Laimbeer as a fisherman: "Laimbeer goes into the lake, looking for salmon, and when his line breaks, he throws a fit, jumps up and down, splashes the water, screams and hollers—and the fish are so scared they just jump into his boat. 'Here! Take us! Just don't hurt us!'"

Sportswriter Brian Schmitz, on what a "Bill Laimbeer doll" would be like if anyone ever made one: "Cries, whines and falls over at the slightest bit of contact. Yells 'Me, ref?' when the string is pulled."

Laimbeer once said that Notre Dame coach Digger Phelps was "shellshocked" at making the 1978 Final Four, and that was why Duke beat the Irish, for which Laimbeer played. Said Phelps in response: "Mike Gminski had an outstanding game against us. Check out who guarded him."

Sportswriter Tim Sullivan, speculating about watching the NBA finals on pay-per-view television: "The NBA finals is worth about $10 per game unless it involves Michael Jordan ($20) or Bill Laimbeer ($2)."

"Laimbeer, who at 35 runs the court as nimbly as a three-legged buffalo, didn't extend interviewing courtesy to local scribes. He hit one of six shots from the floor in 29 minutes of action, so perhaps his play speaks for itself."
> — Portland sportswriter *Kerry Eggers*, after Laimbeer refused to speak to the press following a Trail Blazer thrashing of the Pistons

"Bill Laimbeer is not a candidate for the basketball Hall of Fame unless the Hall adds a jerk wing."
—*Jan Hubbard*, columnist

"Bill is really a good-hearted person. It's just that he has no conscience."
—*Isiah Thomas*

Bill Laimbeer Looks in the Mirror and Sees Truth

"I'll never be small or cuddly. I might as well play my part when I come to Boston Garden. If I gave 60 points on defense, the fans at Boston Garden would still think I'm a fuck. If I were somebody else looking at me, I'd think I was a fuck."
—*Bill Laimbeer*

On the Suitability of Bill Laimbeer Playing for the U.S. Olympic Basketball Team

"Detroit center Bill Laimbeer was considering seeking an injunction against the Olympic selection process because he was deprived of a chance to make the team. Laimbeer said that as a tax-paying citizen, he should have had the opportunity to try out for the team. It would have been great if he could have tried out for the team, because then he would have been excluded on merit rather than logic."
—*Jan Hubbard*

"They shouldn't have tryouts. If they did, Bill Laimbeer wouldn't have even been invited to the tryouts."
—*Charles Barkley*

"Bill Laimbeer couldn't make the Czechoslovakian Olympic team. In 9 million years he couldn't make our Olympic team."
—*Frank Layden*, Utah Jazz president and former NBA coach

And While We're on the Subject, Should Isiah Thomas Have Been Picked for the Olympics Instead of John Stockton?

"Isiah's a cheap-shot artist and if he plays on the Olympic team, I won't."
—*Scottie Pippen*

"Some other guys got left off the team and they're not sitting around whining and complaining. Just for the record, I don't know if Isiah Thomas is as good a player at this point in his career as John Stockton is."
—*Charles Barkley*

"The committee has said to me that Isiah must prove himself again next year, while others can have a horrible year but they are still members of our Olympic team. This is ridiculous because we are penalizing perhaps the greatest small man ever to play the game."
—*Jack McCloskey*, Pistons GM who resigned from the Olympic selection committee in protest over its decision not to pick Thomas

"John Stockton will deliver the ball. That's what John Stockton does better than anyone, and that's what the committee was looking for. I'm not sure they knew Isiah would do that. Is everybody afraid to say this to Isiah's face? I don't know. But I'd tell him. I'd say, 'Because of your actions, nobody likes you. We see through the smiles. We see through all the baloney. We don't want you on our team.' "
—*Frank Layden*

The Rap Against Isiah

Besides the fact that he won't pass the ball, lots of people around the NBA simply don't like Isiah Thomas—"a talented little twit," Mike Lupica calls him. Others have called him much worse. After the Pistons sent Adrian Dantley to Dallas in that big 1989 trade for Isiah's longtime buddy Mark Aguirre, A.D. blamed Thomas for engineering the deal behind the scenes. "I'll never forgive you for what you did to me," Dantley told him. A.D.'s mom was even blunter: "You shouldn't blame [Detroit general manager] Jack McCloskey. He's not the one. It's that little con artist you've got up there. When his royal highness wants something, he gets it."

That seems to be the rap against Isiah—that he's two-faced, that behind that charming smile of his, he's trying to figure a way to take advantage; he's a Machiavelli in gym shorts. It was reportedly Isiah who spread the rumors that Magic Johnson was bisexual and had contracted AIDS through gay sex, thus contributing to Magic's decision not to pursue a comeback. You can't be sure about anything with Isiah, not even when he supposedly gets hurt. "I'm not going to say they [the Pistons] exaggerate his injuries," said Detroit beat writer Steve Addy. "But let's put it this way: It's good theater for them to make his injuries look as bad as possible. Then when he takes the court: It's a miracle! He's back! Another Isiah miracle, brought to you by the Detroit Pistons."

For years as leader of the Bad Boys, Isiah has committed "lowdown thuggery" (Mike Lupica's phrase) on teams around the league, particularly his archrivals Michael Jordan and the Chicago Bulls. It's said that the feud between the two superstars goes back to the 1985 All Star Game when Isiah, the veteran point guard, kept the ball away from the rookie Jordan to teach him a lesson and keep him in his place. Spurred by their bruising on-court battles, their animosity steadily grew over the years, with the two of them sniping periodically at each other. There was talk one year of staging a $1 million pay-per-view one-on-one game between Magic Johnson and Michael Jordan, but Thomas, as president of the players' association, scotched the idea. Asked about why he might have done this, Jordan said, "I wonder what Isiah's position would be if he were playing Magic. But, of course, if he were playing Magic, no one would want to see it."

Jordan was once asked why Isiah and the other Detroit guards weren't faring well in the fan voting for the NBA All Star team. "I don't think the Detroit guys are having good years," said Jordan.

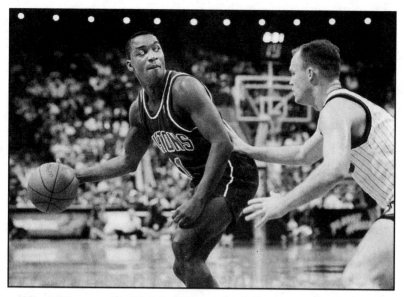

His critics say that Isiah Thomas is shifty not only on the basketball court, but off it, too. (Photo by Joe Gosen)

"Besides, people don't like Detroit." On yet another occasion, while analyzing the reasons for Detroit's success, Jordan tossed another barb their way: "They dirty up the game of basketball. Sportsmanship should always be a part of sport, but they have taken that away. Now other teams want to play that way because of their success."

While Jordan and Thomas have lately made a well-publicized attempt to patch up their differences, the bad feelings about Isiah linger around the league. Some people even thought that Karl Malone's elbow to Isiah's head in 1991—sending him to the hospital and knocking him out of the lineup—was a payback of sorts for all the bad things he and the Bad Boys had done over the years. But Charles Barkley said this wasn't the case. "Nobody wants to put 40 stitches in a guy's head," he explained. "Not even Isiah's."

Isiah's Accomplice

The trade may have broken Adrian Dantley's heart, but many Piston followers think that getting Mark Aguirre in that 1989 trade was the final piece of the puzzle that Detroit needed to become a championship team. While Detroit may have been rejoicing, nobody in Dallas was exactly sad to see Aguirre go. "There was a night-and-day difference in practice today," Mavericks forward Sam Perkins said after Aguirre left. "Today should be an all-day party. I will never understand Mark. Maybe he has a chemical imbalance."

A chemical imbalance? Maybe that's the reason for Aguirre's Danny Ainge–type whining. Observes sportswriter Jeff Weinstock: "An Aguirre on-court pout looks so close to actual crying that you want to lob him a hankie. Or, better, a pacifier. Shaddup!" Aguirre whines off the court, too. After the Pistons signed Orlando Woolridge to a big extension but refused to renegotiate Aguirre's contract, he cried foul. "To be looked over is insulting. They [the Pistons] just bypassed me. What gets me is that I feel they have really underestimated my talents. And you tell me: I'm not as valuable as some other individual? You'd have to be blind not to see there is a clear injustice being done."

Like fellow Bad Boy Bill Laimbeer, Aguirre also thought that there was an injustice in the way the players on the U.S. Olympic Dream Team were picked. He said he was so incensed that he was tempted to try out for another country's Olympic squad. Which drew this reaction from sportswriter Norm Clarke: "So the Pistons' Mark Aguirre, the temperamental one, is thinking about playing on the Mexican Olympic basketball team? How do you say 'stiff' in Spanish?"

How Do You Stop Michael Jordan?
A Bad Boy Explains . . .

"You go to church—and when you're playing him you try to talk about things Michael doesn't like to talk about. Like baldness."
—*John Salley*

What the Bad Boys Think of Michael Jordan

"Michael portrays the image of an angel, but he's no angel. Anyone who has gotten as far as he has in this game has popped a few people along the way, and Michael has popped more than a few people."

> —*Mark Aguirre*

"All he does is play basketball. In the world he's this big."

> —*Bill Laimbeer*, holding his fingers an inch apart

"There is not one guy who sets the tone on our team. That's what makes us a team. If one guy did everything, we wouldn't be a team. We'd be the Chicago Bulls."

> —*John Salley*, mocking Jordan and the Bulls during the Detroit Pistons' championship years

"We don't care who scores the points as long as we win. It would be hard for Michael Jordan to play on this team because he's got to score all the points. I don't think he'd fit in here."

> —*John Salley*

"They may have the best player, but we have the best team."

> —*Bill Laimbeer*, with another needle for Jordan's Bulls

. . . And What They Thought of Larry Bird

"He's a smart player. I give him all the credit in the world. He takes advantage of his strengths. He can read picks, and he can go around picks for dish-offs, but other than that he's a decent player. He ain't God, he ain't the best player in the league."

> —*Dennis Rodman*, after Bird's Celtics beat the Pistons in the bitterly contested 1987 Eastern Conference finals

"He's white. That's the only reason he gets it. I don't care. . . . Go right ahead and tell him."

> —more from *Dennis Rodman*, on why Bird won three MVP awards

"I think Larry Bird is a very, very good basketball player, an exceptional talent, but I have to agree with Rodman. If he were black, he'd be just another good guy."
—*Isiah Thomas*

The Storm That Followed

Spoken as they were in the aftermath of a bitterly disappointing playoff loss, Rodman's and Thomas's comments about Bird caused a ruckus of considerable proportions. Rodman was a rookie and little known then. But Isiah was one of the NBA's premier players, and his remarks carried more weight. So much weight, in fact, it almost buried him.

In the days that followed, the Pistons' point guard was accused of being a sore loser and worse, a black bigot. The attack on his character was blistering, and Isiah sought to defend himself and explain his remarks further in an interview with Ira Berkow of *The New York Times*.

"When Bird makes a great play," Thomas told Berkow, "it's due to his thinking and his work habits. It's not the case for blacks. All we do is run and jump. We never practice or give a thought to how we play. It's like I came dribbling out of my mother's womb. It's like we're animals, lions and tigers, who run around wild in a jungle."

Referring to Bird's dramatic theft and pass to a streaking Dennis Johnson that stole a last-second win for the Celtics in game five of the series, Thomas went on, "This white guy on the other team who is supposed to be very slow, with little coordination, who can't jump, all of a sudden appears out of nowhere, jumps in, grabs the ball, leaps up in the air as he's falling out of bounds, looks over the court and in the space of two or three seconds, picks out a player cutting for the basket with a picture-perfect pass to win the game. You tell me this white guy—Bird—did that with no God-given talent?"

But the issue did not die down despite these remarks, and the NBA felt compelled to call a press conference of its own so that Bird himself could say that no, he didn't think Isiah was a racist and yes, he was sure that as a basketball player, Isiah thought he was "bad." Bird said that Isiah apologized to him but didn't need to, and he tried to make a joke out of it. "The only thing I've got to say is that Isiah should know better than to listen to Rodman. You never agree with a rookie."

The incident finally blew over, but for black players at least, there was a cautionary moral to what happened to Isiah. "You can't say anything about Larry Bird," said Knicks center Jawann Oldham. "That's like saying something about the Grand Wizard himself."

The Boston Celtics: The Green, White, and Red Franchise

The green is for Celtic green, the color of the most famous team in basketball and the one with more championship banners than any other. The team of Russell, the Jones brothers, Havlicek, Cowens, DJ, Parish, Kevin McHale, Bird, and so many more. The white is for, well, white, as in honky. For many years the Celtics have had the reputation around the NBA as the team with more white players on it than any other. And the red is, of course, for Red Auerbach, the man who, as coach and general manager, built the Boston Celtics into one of the greatest franchises in sports history.

Red's Wisdom

In Boston, he's a hero. Outside of Boston, well, the reviews are more mixed. But Red Auerbach was indisputably the driving force behind all those championship banners that are hanging from the rafters at creaky old Boston Garden. With all his success on the basketball courts, both as a championship coach and a general manager, he is a much sought-after speaker at business and civic functions. Here, then, are some pearls of wisdom from Arnold Auerbach:

On succeeding in business: "I gave a speech the other day on how to gain the competitive edge. I told them, 'You're paying me for nothing. I can give the whole speech in a word. Cheat! Here's how you do it. In hockey, got a slow team? Have soft ice. In football, got a slow team? Let the grass grow. In baseball? Fool around with the height of the mound. In basketball? Loosen the rims. Hell, lower the rims if you have to."

On the value of experience: "Experience don't mean shit."

No less an authority than Red Auerbach said that Larry Bird was the greatest of all Boston Celtics—before his back acted up, of course. (Photo by Joe Gosen)

On teaching and coaching: "Remember—it's not what you tell them, but what they hear."

On why he wouldn't cave in to the salary demands of a player: "Hey, how much ass can you kiss? Then the guy owns you. I'm not crazy."

To his players, when he was both coach and general manager of the Celtics: "If you guys don't like the way I run things, go see the GM. I'll be there an hour after practice."

On being the man in charge: "You know what *boss* spelled backwards is? Double S-O-B."

On why he wasn't going to draft Holy Cross basketball star Bob Cousy in 1950: "I don't give a damn for sentiment or names. That goes for Cousy and everybody else. The only thing that counts with me is ability and Cousy still hasn't proven to me that he's got that ability. I'm not interested in drafting someone just because he happens to be a local yokel." (Auerbach later changed his mind and was glad he did.)

On his critics: "When you're winning, and you've been around as long as I was, more than any other coach, they're always looking for angles to get you. Anything to put you down, say something derogatory about you. It's a form of jealousy, so I dismissed it."

On being associated with the Boston franchise: "The Celtics aren't a team, they're a way of life."

Others Talk About Red

For all his wisdom and experience, Red is hardly a beloved figure outside Massachusetts. In fact, a lot of the people who coached and played against him over the years think he's a rat. They accuse him of being a cheat who is always looking to take unfair advantage of his opponents, a guy who steals ideas and claims them as his own, a guy who doesn't turn on the air conditioning in the opposing team's locker room when they come to Boston Garden, among many other underhanded deeds.

"I always thought that Red would be the type of guy who, if he was standing on the streetcorner and some kid came up to him for

an autograph, he'd say, 'Who asked you to come over here?'"
>—*Paul Seymour*, who coached against Auerbach for the Syracuse Nationals in the 1950s

"You got the feeling that Red wanted certain rules just because it would be better for him, and forget about the league."
>—*Daniel Biasone*, ex-owner of the Syracuse Nationals

"I played and coached in the NBA and things haven't changed from when I was in the league. He was the biggest mouth in the league then and he still is."
>—*Slick Leonard*, coach of the Indiana Pacers of the old ABA, after Auerbach said that Julius Erving was "not a great player"

"The way it works up there, is that whatever goes right Red did. Whatever goes wrong, the owner did."
>—Kentuckian *John Y. Brown*, former Celtics owner

"For 38 years, the essential duties of a Celtic owner have been to kiss Red's ring, sign the checks, and be ready to accept the championship trophy."
>—*Bob Cousy*, past Celtic great

"If he took your idea, it was his idea."
>—Celtic front-office employee, as quoted by the *Hartford Courant*

Red's Cigar

Auerbach's trademark was his cigar. As coach, sitting on the bench, after the Celtics had a big game wrapped up, he'd light up a victory cigar. It was his statement that the game was over, even though the players might still be playing and time might still be left on the clock. It used to drive people nuts. What may have made them really mad was the fact that Auerbach lit up so many cigars, so often.

"He sat benignly and comfortably on the bench, smoking away, with a guard behind him. Meanwhile, we were out on the floor taking all this abuse. The feeling among the Celtic players was, 'Why get their [fans'] attention any more? Why piss 'em off?' The fans would get more belligerent and hostile towards us, and we had to bust our tails to keep the lead because once he went for the cigar, the other team's intensity went up 100 percent. I hated that thing."
—*Bob Cousy*

"A self-aggrandizing gimmick even his own players hated."
—*Harvey Araton* and *Filip Bondy*, on Red's cigar habit

"To be truthful, in those days most of us would love to have shoved that cigar right down his throat."
—*Dolph Schayes*, former Celtic opponent

How Red Got His Nickname

"We're not making this up: Theodore 'Blue' Edwards [of the Utah Jazz] was nicknamed when an older sister found the 1-year-old choking on a baby bottle in his crib. We are making this up: Red Auerbach was nicknamed when an older sister caught 10-year-old Arnold sucking on a baby bottle in someone else's crib."
—*Rotisserie League Basketball*

Boston Garden, Shrine of Basketball

In addition to the Machiavellian intrigues of Red Auerbach, one thing that Celtic teams could always count on over the years was their home-court advantage. Going to Boston Garden is like stepping back into basketball's past. Every NBA team used to play in arenas like the Garden; the difference is, they all tore *theirs* down.

"Man, my driveway is better than this."
—Cleveland guard *Ron Harper*, surveying the Garden's famed but somewhat erratic parquet floor

"There is no mystique."
—*Gene Shue*, visiting basketball coach

"If you've played basketball for 15 or 20 years, you started in a sweaty little gym like Boston Garden. You should be used to this sort of thing. But once you get to the summertime, it's not someplace you want to be."
—*James Worthy*, Lakers forward

"A trash compactor for Laker basketball teams."
—columnist *Scott Ostler*, summing up the Garden from the Los Angeles point of view

"There are guys doing 25 years to life who would refuse to come in here."
—Detroit assistant coach *Brendan Malone*, surveying a locker room in the Garden where the Pistons had to dress before a championship game with the Celtics

"This room! Oh no, not this room!"
—*Dennis Rodman*, upon entering the same room

An Old Celtic Point Guard Makes Two Points

Is Bob Cousy, one of the greatest Celtics ever and the second greatest point guard of all time, getting a little cranky in his old age? Based on a couple of his recent statements, you be the judge.

Cousy on point guard Sherman Douglas: "Where are the skills? They're not really discernible. I'm told he'll grow on you—that he has to get maximum minutes to run the show, but if that's the truth, that might never happen. He doesn't look like an exceptional point guard."

Cousy on the state of the game today compared to when he played: "If you're talking about Hall of Famers, yes, we could play. There are guys today making a million dollars a year who go to applaud and miss their hands. Bill Russell, Oscar Robertson, guys like that—we would function today, and quite effectively, if not actually dominate. Russ would still be effective. I would be one of the premier point guards. Point guards are at much more of a premium. I don't think there are five or six now who can really run a team."

And Bill Russell Reveals Why He Is Not One of the Most Beloved Players of All Time

"I owe the public nothing and I'll pay them nothing. I refuse to smile and be nice to the kiddies."
> —a young Bill Russell, who was guarded and suspicious toward the public early in his career and never changed

Playing in Boston: The Black Perspective

What is it about Boston sports teams, anyway? The baseball Red Sox have historically tended to favor their white players at the expense of blacks, while the same would appear to be true with the basketball Celtics. Black players dominate on every other NBA team, but in Beantown there are all these stubby little white guys running around. What gives? Here is the black perspective on what it means to play for the Celtics.

"To me, the Celtics represent white supremacy."
> —*Spike Lee*, filmmaker

"To me, Boston itself was a flea market of racism. . . . If Paul Revere were riding today, it would be for racism: 'The niggers are coming! The niggers are coming!' he'd yell as he galloped through town to warn neighbors of busing and black homeowners."
> —*Bill Russell*, writing in his autobiography, 1979

"If you're a black Celtic, as long as you're producing, you're accepted. But if you're not, then you are just a black."
> —*Cedric Maxwell*, former Celtic forward

"You know, Maxwell, you remind me of that old movie guy, Stepin Fetchit."

> —the reported words of *Red Auerbach* to Cedric Maxwell, at a 1978 team Christmas party

"I love the guy. I was hoping I could stretch the thing out as long as I could, because I was hoping and hoping these monkeys could turn it around."

> —more insensitive comments from Auerbach, explaining why he had to fire former Celtic standout Tom Heinsohn as coach of a black-dominated Boston squad

"Whenever we'd lose, they'd use a big picture of me or Robert [Parish] or Max [Cedric Maxwell] on sports. Check it out. When we won, they'd use Larry [Bird] or Kevin [McHale] or Danny [Ainge], but when we'd lose it'd be one of us."

> —*Dennis Johnson*, on Boston's newspaper coverage of the team during the 1980s

"Let me put it this way. Management is aware of the city. Red was always smart enough to understand [racism] is there. Red plays the hand that's dealt him. That's why Red's always tried to keep it even—six whites, six blacks, maybe seven to five. No matter what they'd say for the record, it was always assumed there had to be a certain amount of whites on the team. . . . You'd start with the blacks you knew would make it and figured everyone else would be white."

> —*JoJo White*, who played 10 years for the Celtics

"They try to recruit the best white guys who play the game. They're catering to the paying fans. It's a format that's worked for them for years. Why go against it, especially if it's accepted by white society?"

> —*Gerald Henderson*, former Celtic playoff hero

"There is an air of hostility here that doesn't exist in any other big city in America. I don't know how to explain it, except to say

that you're uncomfortable here. I was with Bob Lanier, the former Piston, recently. He said, 'How can you stand this town?' I don't know. It's just uncomfortable. I go to Providence, to Hartford, and I never feel uncomfortable. They're not very far away. It's just different here."
> —*Ken Hudson*, a black executive with the Celtics, on what it's like to be a black in Boston

"It's an Irish town. If they could have five guys named O'Reilly, they'd be in great shape."
> —*Ron Grinker*, player agent

"It wasn't a secret. It was obvious. You look at the endorsements up there. In all the years I played, I never got one offer. The year I won the MVP, nothing. You had white players who barely played in commercials."
> —*Cedric Maxwell*

"It seemed to me up there the black players in Boston weren't people. We were like machines. If we worked out, fine. If not, treat 'em like shit."
> —*Sidney Wicks*, ex–UCLA star who played in Boston

"If you were a black player and you were drawing what management thought was a good salary, and you sprained an ankle, you were expected to hurry back before the injury was healed. One of us got hurt it was, 'Put some ice on it and be out there the next day.' If you said anything it was, 'Hey, we pay you to do a job.' Then it comes out in the papers and you're the bad guy. But if, say, Havlicek sprained an ankle, he was told to go take a holiday."
> —*JoJo White*

"The black players would always joke around. We'd say, 'If there's a black person in the crowd, you can find him fast because he's the one yelling, 'Peanuts! Peanuts! Get your peanuts!' "
> —*Cedric Maxwell*, on the racially homogeneous crowds at Boston Garden

"Everyone turned white. For a minute there, we looked like the Celtics."

> —a Laker player, after the team plane encountered a midflight storm that knocked some people out of their seats

Dolph Schayes Shows That You Don't Have to Be Black to Hate the Celtics

One of the greatest players in the early days of the NBA, Dolph Schayes, was a confirmed Celtics hater. He played for the old Syracuse Nationals in the 1950s and he just couldn't stand those Boys in Green. He thought they were arrogant and that Auerbach and Co. would cheat, bite, steal—whatever it took—to win. "For us, we just hated the Celtics," he said once. "They were the guys in the green shirts that nobody liked. If they were walking down the street, we'd walk down the other side." For Celtics haters everywhere, Schayes is a kind of inspiration. What he shows is that hatred of the Celtics transcends not only time, but ethnic and racial boundaries as well. When he was 60, Schayes showed up at a 1988 NBA Old-Timer's Game and watched ex-Celtic center Dave Cowens push somebody out of the way to grab a rebound and put back a shot to win the game. "Nothing ever changes in this goddamned league," said a disgusted Schayes afterward. "The Celtics are going to find a way to cheat or do something to win."

A Celtic Sampler: From the Seventies

The Boston Celtics are the most successful franchise in NBA history, but they don't *always* win. There was a particularly bleak period in the mid- to late 1970s, when they featured such players as Sidney Wicks and Curtis Rowe. The former UCLA stars may have shined at Pauley Pavilion, but they couldn't cut it at Boston Garden. Rowe, at least, had the kind of attitude that could carry him through all those tough times and losing games. "Hey, man," he said once, "there are no W's and L's on the paycheck." That's right, Curtis. *The bank don't care.*

Reporters once asked Celtic mainstay Kevin McHale for his prediction for the upcoming season. "Listen," said McHale, "if I could look into the future, I wouldn't be sitting here talking to you doorknobs. I'd be out investing in the stock market." (Photo by Brad Mangin)

This post-Havlicek, pre-Bird era is regarded as something of a dark age by Celtic fans, and is memorable for no other reason than Bob Ryan's classic summation of the team during the period: "The Celtics used to stand for something. Now all they stand for is the anthem."

A Celtic Sampler: From the Eighties

Then they drafted Bird, and everything changed. Along with the Los Angeles Lakers, the Boston Celtics were one of the two premier teams of the 1980s. They had some great teams and great players run up and down that rickety old parquet floor. A sampling of quotes and comments from that time:

"I can't come out here [on the court] for a game smiling and joking. To me this is serious, and I have to give my complete attention."
> —the young *Larry Bird*, comparing himself with another rookie who entered the NBA in 1979, Magic Johnson

"Let him eat spaghetti."
> —Celtic coach *Bill Fitch*, on hearing that Boston's number-one draft pick in 1980, Kevin McHale, was going to Italy and thinking about signing with a pro team there

"I miss waking up every morning knowing I'm going to kick somebody's ass."
> —*Bill Walton*, who came to the Celtics in the mid-eighties and helped them win an NBA championship in 1985–86, on what he missed upon his retirement from basketball

"I've been in the league six years, and I've never seen him play a game. I saw some film of him once, but it was on a black and white television."
> —*Kevin McHale*, joking about the oft-injured Walton when he first joined the team

"They used to compare Danny Ainge to Jerry West. So much for comparisons."

> —the sharp-tongued *Kevin McHale*, on his former Celtic teammate

"They used to compare Kevin to Herman Munster. Guess they were right."

> —*Danny Ainge*, responding to McHale's remark about him

"You know what I like to do in the off season? I like to get in my big fancy car, drive around to construction sites, and watch guys work. Then I roll down the window and say, 'Guess what, boys? I got nothing to do today.' "

> —*Cedric Maxwell*, Celtics forward

"Before Kevin McHale hit Kurt Rambis, the Lakers were just running across the street whenever they wanted. Now they stop at the corner, push the button, wait for the light, and look both ways."

> —*Cedric Maxwell*, after McHale belted the Lakers forward on a fast break during game four of the 1984 Los Angeles–Boston finals (considered the turning point of the series, the incident propelled Boston to a seven-game comeback win)

"Arnold, you're showing me all the class I knew you had."

> —referee *Earl Strom*, after general manager Auerbach came down from his seat in the stands to berate Strom during the 1987 finals against Los Angeles

"Here is a guy who has never done one contract. I mean, what can this guy tell them, or promise he can do compared to some of the top agents in the game? What does he have, a spell over these guys or something?"

> —*Red Auerbach*, on player agent Jerome Stanley, who engaged in a bitter salary dispute with Auerbach at the end of the decade regarding young Celtic stars Reggie Lewis and Brian Shaw

"He's white, he smokes cigars, he's supposed to represent some intelligence."

> —*Jerome Stanley*, on what he knew about Auerbach

"Street-smart city slickers who hustled the Celtics with a con game."

> —broadcaster *Will McDonough*, on Reggie Lewis and Jerome Stanley after Stanley negotiated a big contract extension for Lewis

"That was an absolute disgrace to the game of basketball for guys in Celtics uniforms to go out and play like that. There was no effort, no anything. You guys [reporters] have to write about it. I had to endure watching it."

> —Celtic coach *Chris Ford*, after a 1991 loss to the lowly Denver Nuggets

"Last time when they beat us, Bird was talking a lot on the floor. A lot of them were talking a lot of trash. Even when we get blowed up, they should not talk like that. I didn't see nobody talking tonight."

> —Nuggets center *Dikembe Mutombo*, after the same game

"The Celtics have no shot at another title unless the team can find a way to train at Lourdes."

> —sportswriter *George Shirk*, assessing Boston's chances as their once-formidable front line of McHale, Bird, and Parish grew older and slower

Two Early and Somewhat Premature Assessments of Larry Bird Before He Entered the NBA

"He's slow and deficient. . . . He could be an excellent goalie on a zone defense but he may develop a sore neck watching faster forwards speed past him."

> —a writer, assessing the prospects of Indiana State's Larry Bird as he prepared for his rookie year in the NBA

"Boy, is he slow. . . . It's a shame he couldn't be as quick as the other guys out there."
—Lakers GM *Jerry West,* on the same subject

Larry Legend

Bird, of course, made fools of his early critics and became (according to no less an authority than Red Auerbach) the greatest Boston Celtic of all time, greater even than the great Bill Russell. One of the keys to Bird's greatness may have been that, despite being a shy, small-town boy from French Lick, Indiana, he never lacked for confidence on a basketball court. As a matter of fact he could talk trash with the best of those city slickers from New York and Detroit.

There are plenty of examples of this, but few can match Bird's Clash of the Titans confrontation with Julius Erving at the start of the 1984–85 season. Bird just performed surgery on the Doctor, outscoring him at will and showing him up all over the court. The two began taunting each other and gradually the taunts turned to shoves and the shoves into a fight. Both were fined a whopping $7,500 apiece for their behavior in a game the Celtics—and Bird, in his individual matchup against Erving—won easily. Bird poured in 42 points to Erving's 6, and supposedly Bird ran down the court taunting the Doctor, "Forty-two to 6, 42 to 6," before their fight broke out.

Bird was cocky as a rooster. You have to be to take on someone like Doctor J. Before an All Star Game three-point shooting contest one year, an official came into the locker room where the contestants were gathered and said that they wanted the winner to come to center court after the event was over. Bird spoke up, "How long do you want me out there?" He wasn't kidding. He won the shoot-out.

After CBS delayed an NBA finals game because the network did not want to compete for viewers with the Indianapolis 500, which was occurring that same day, an angry Bird said, "Heck, I'm bigger than the Indianapolis 500—even in Indiana." He may have been right.

In one of those Celtic–Piston playoff games of a few years ago when they went after each other with hammer and tongs, Isiah Thomas was tearing the place up, scoring on the Celtic guards like they weren't even there. Bird confronted him. "Are you finished yet?" he demanded. "No," said Isiah. "Well, you're through now, because it's my turn," said Bird. Bird did indeed take his turn and led the Celtics to a comeback win.

Another great example of Bird taking a shot—and then giving one back—occurred in the 1981 finals against Moses Malone and the Houston Rockets. With the series tied at two games apiece, Moses chose what would seem to be a rather unpropitious moment to verbally dump on his opponents. "I could get four guys off the streets of Petersburg, Virginia [his hometown], and beat them," he told the media. "I don't think they're all that good. I don't think they can stop us from doing what we want to do." Even after the Celtics beat the Rockets in the fifth game by 29 points, Moses would not change his opinion: "The Celtics are still chumps," he said. "I'm speaking from the heart now, and I want everybody to understand. I have respect for those guys, but they just aren't that good. If we play our game, they can't beat us. Tonight we didn't play our game. The Celtics aren't going to drink champagne after game six, they'll drink Gatorade to get their strength back."

But Moses was wrong. The Celtics popped the bubbly after game six, having won the world title. A few days later tens of thousands of people came out to a victory celebration on the streets of Boston to honor the team. In the crowd one fellow held up a sign that said MOSES EATS SHIT, which was spotted by one of the Celtic speakers at the rally. "You're right," said Larry Bird, to the horror and delight of the thousands. "Moses does eat shit."

Larry Meets the Rifleman

Larry Bird also had some great in-your-face-offs with former Indiana Pacer forward Chuck Person, who's quite a talker himself. Person is a flighty character—"If Chuck just went out and played the game he'd be all right," says a former teammate, "but when he thinks too much he gets into trouble, because none of us know where his brain is"—but he always seemed to pick up his game and his trash-talking when he faced Bird and the Celtics. One time when Boston came to Market Square Arena in Indianapolis, Person sought Bird out before the game and said to him, "Larry, we have 16,530 people in here. We've been averaging about 13. Three thousand people came to see you. The other 13,000 came to see me. This is my house. I'm going to control it."

Sometimes he did, sometimes he didn't. But it always made for great theater. Person, aka the Rifleman, was at his lip-shooting best during the 1991 Indiana–Boston playoff series. Though only a first-round series, it was a barn-burner, and Person was running around setting fires wherever he could. After scoring 12 points in a row at one point in a game, he ran down the court shouting, "Nobody can guard me! Nobody! I'm a bad man!" Considering it was number 33 for the Celtics who was guarding him—or attempting to, as Person joked—this ranks on a trash-talking par with Bird's own "Forty-two to 6" taunting of Doctor J. Here are some other Person-isms from that series:

After firing in a high-trajectory three-pointer: "I shot it as high as I could, so everyone could admire it."

On talking trash to Bird: "Larry knew I was in his ear, now I'm going to be in his dreams."

On being guarded by Kevin McHale and Bird: "I knew when Larry and McHale got on me, the shots were going in. It's like I was out there for target practice, shooting H-O-R-S-E by myself."

And, regarding the prospect of returning to Boston for the fifth and final game of the series: "Unless they come up with something different, we're going to go tear some of that parquet up in Boston."

On this last count, however, the Rifleman misfired. The Celtics won that game and the series, leaving the final word about their duel to the Bird. "Yeah, it is a little sweeter, I guess, since we beat Chuck. We've had a lot of good battles. But it always seems like I get the last word."

Larry Tightwad

Larry Bird may or may not have been the greatest white basketball player of all time, but he certainly was the cheapest. "The most incredible thing I ever saw Larry Bird do was pick up a check in a restaurant once," said one-time Celtic teammate M. L. Carr. Bird

Chuck Person used to light it up—with both his mouth and his outside shooting—whenever he faced another good trash-talker, Larry Bird. (Photo courtesy of the Indiana Pacers)

struggled for years with a bad back before calling it quits in 1992. His many admirers said that despite his injuries Bird kept playing because of his love for the game, not because of all the money the Celtics were paying him. Boston sportswriter Dan Shaughnessy knew better. "This isn't the Larry Bird I know," he said. "Bad back or no, he'd dive into the aisle of an airplane if he saw a dime on the carpet."

Bird's status as a Hall of Fame penny-pincher was demonstrated when the Dream Team stopped in ritzy Monaco to practice before the Barcelona Olympics. After being served a beer, Bird asked the waiter how much it cost in American dollars. French Lick's only millionaire was aghast. "You can keep your $7 beer," he said, and shoved the glass back.

Larry Quipster

Larry Bird was never as engaging with the public or the media as his friend, rival, and counterpart Magic Johnson. Nevertheless, he had a sly, Indiana country-boy sense of humor that sometimes took people by surprise. Some examples:

On being told that Bill Laimbeer didn't make the All Star team with him: "Good, now I won't have to get on the bus on game day and have him say, 'Hi, Larry,' and then I have to say, 'Fuck you, Bill.' "

After being informed that *Esquire* magazine had picked him as one of the "Young Leaders of America": "Yeah, sure. Me and Cyndi Lauper."

On breaking into the NBA with gawky Rick Robey as one of his teammates: "When I got to rookie camp, I realized I could play in this league. The thing about it is, I had Rick Robey guarding me, so I probably thought I was gonna be a little bit better than I really was."

While a senior at Indiana State, at a press conference about a newspaper columnist who had attacked him and his team: "Is David Israel here? Too bad. I always did want to see what a real live prick looked like."

On a fight in the 1986 NBA finals between Boston's 6'1" Jerry Sichting and Houston's 7'4" Ralph Sampson: "I can't believe he picked a fight with Sichting. Heck, my girlfriend could beat him up."

At the 1986 NBA All Star game, Bird won the three-point shooting competition, while the 6'1" Isiah Thomas won the game MVP and 5'7" Spud Webb won the slam dunk contest. Said Bird after the event: "This was the week of the brilliant and short people. I was brilliant. The rest of the people were short."

Reporter: "How come every time I see you talking on these television commercials you sound so smart and smooth, but in person you sound like such a douche bag?"

Bird (laughing): "Because they pay me to talk."

With the Celtics up 3–1 against the 76ers in the 1985 Eastern Conference finals and going home to Boston for the next game, a Philly fan yelled out at Bird as he was leaving the floor: "See you next Friday [for game six]." Responded Bird: "You have a better chance of seeing God." (The Celtics won the game and did not return to Philadelphia.)

After the Celtics choked in a playoff game loss to the Lakers, a disgusted Bird was asked what it would take to turn things around for Boston. He responded: "Twelve heart transplants."

When asked by a reporter what he liked to do when he wasn't playing basketball, Bird said, "Play basketball." (Okay, it's not exactly an insult, but it does pretty nicely sum up Bird's personality and the nature of his appeal.)

And Now That He's Retired, Who Should Play Bird in the Movie?

"I'm perfect for it: the right age, close to his height, can play the game a little and can definitely be that ugly—all I need is a really bad hairdo and a bad mustache and I'm in."

—actor Daniel (*Home Alone*) Stern, suggesting that he could play the title role if Hollywood ever makes *The Larry Bird Story*

Mr. Outrageous, Charles Barkley

To borrow an old Buddy Hackett line about Howard Cosell, there have always been mixed emotions about Charles Barkley. Some people hate him like poison—and some people hate him just regular. But that's not entirely true. In fact, there are many people who are actually quite fond of the voluble Mr. B. Whatever your opinion, one thing is certainly true: The NBA would be a lot less interesting without him.

Charles Talks . . . and Talks . . . and Talks

Charles Barkley is a great basketball player, but his most impressive attribute may be his mouth. It's going all the time, and media people love it because Charles himself doesn't seem to have much control over it. Here are some recent utterances from the Mouth That Keeps Roaring:

Charles, on how most basketball fans see him: "If I weren't earning more than $3 million a year to dunk a basketball, most people on the street would run in the other direction if they saw me coming."

On why he's such good friends with Michael Jordan: "We're friends because most of the guys in this league are jerks and you wouldn't want to spend any time with them."

On what he thought of Larry Bird's skills as a defensive player: "As long as he's around, I'll only be the second-worst defensive player in basketball."

On his standing in basketball: "I don't think there's any doubt. Anybody in their right mind knows I'm the best forward in basketball. Well, the only person comparable to me is Karl Malone, but his body is so different from mine. Even my wife loves his body, and that's the main reason I say I'm the best. With a body like that he is supposed to be awesome. With a body like mine, I'm supposed to be a couch potato."

On changing his uniform number from 34 to 32, in honor of Magic Johnson: "This isn't about anything but me and Earvin. It's about a friend. I don't give a shit what people think. People are stupid."

On finishing second to Magic in the 1990 MVP balloting: "It's not like it's a shock to me that I did not win. I did not expect to win. You have to realize this is a business, and I'm not the most popular business guy."

More realistic thoughts from Charles: "I wouldn't want to be a diplomat. I want to be Charles. I'm gonna be real. I'm what life is about. I don't play games or put up fronts. I don't tell people what they wanna hear. I tell them the truth."

On how he lost weight when he was a young, chubby college player: "I cut down to six meals a day."

On the newly designed uniforms of the Philadelphia 76ers: "They look like my daughter got ahold of some crayons and designed them."

On the NBA preseason: "You can't compare preseason to regular season. Preseason is just a way to screw fans out of money."

On the Indiana Pacers, circa 1991: "They could be scary if they ever learn how to play basketball, which they haven't yet."

On what it's like to play against the spectator-sparse New Jersey Nets: "When you play New Jersey, it's just you, the Nets, and a few of your closest friends."

On his rebounding technique: "Yeah, I've got technique. It's called, 'Just Go Get the Damn Ball.' "

On Atlanta's Dominique Wilkins: "He might be the most overrated, overhyped player in the league . . . Until the 1990–91 season he avoided rebounds and assists like they had a disease. He's still not as good as the hype would have you believe. Take away his scoring ability and what do you have?"

On Bucks guard Alvin Robertson: "A hatchet man. Referees let him get away with more hand-checking than a prostitute."

On men who womanize: "These guys who have three or four babies by different women should have their balls cut off."

After NBA commissioner David Stern signed a multimillion-dollar contract: "I should be the commissioner. When I retire, that's my goal. He can't rebound like me, he definitely can't dunk like me, he definitely don't get beat up like me. He gets to wear a suit every day, while I get to run up and down the court, and he makes more than me. That's crazy. I need a raise."

On his philosophy of life: "Life's got to be funny. If you're not enjoying it, you might as well be dead."

Management vs. Charles (I)

Darryl Dawkins once said that Harold Katz is "an owner I wouldn't wish on Dracula." Well, Dracula never suited up for Katz's Philadelphia 76ers, but Charles Barkley did for eight years—and the result was the messiest scene this side of Transylvania.

Here's what Charles said about Katz in his book, *Outrageous*: "One of our problems is that Harold enjoys making deals, and yet he knows about as much about basketball as any fan who sits around watching games all the time—not much." Barkley later blamed his co-author for putting words in his mouth, but Katz wouldn't accept that. "I find it hard to believe you can be misquoted writing your own book," he said.

Katz found it hard to believe Charles had been misquoted because (a) Charles says things like that all the time, and (b) he has said similar things about Katz and his organization before. "The Sixers are gutless," he told one interviewer. "For example, we can't have beer in the locker rooms. I can't have a beer after I run up and down the court for two hours, but they're going to serve it to the guy who's got a wife and two kids to drive home. That is so gutless. They're only concerned about making money." Barkley said that Katz was the reason that attitudes on the Sixers were so crummy: "The only reason we're not as good as we could be is an attitude. If you enjoy playing for an organization, you'll give a little bit more. I don't think anybody enjoys playing for Harold, and that hurts our performance." Barkley criticized Philadelphia for releasing Rick Mahorn and for trading Sixers legend Maurice Cheeks without informing him first. "A TV guy says to Maurice, 'Well, how do you feel about the trade?' and Maurice says, 'What trade?' The guy says, 'You've been traded to New York.' And the tears came to his eyes. I'll never forget that. It burns my heart every day. Here he was, one of the best point guards in basketball for 10 years, and they treat him like that. That's ridiculous."

Barkley's most controversial swipe at Katz was over the Dave Hoppen issue. Barkley said that the only reason geeky Dave was on the team in 1991 was that he was white; if he hadn't been on it, the entire Sixers team would have been made up of African-Americans, and Katz would never tolerate that because of the racism of Philadelphia spectators. The Sixers owner, said Charles, "has to think about his ticket-buyers. There is a certain minority of people out there who are racist, who don't want to see an all-black team, who would complain." Katz was outraged. "Charles does not speak for this team," he said. "He does not speak for the coaches. And he doesn't speak for this owner. I speak for myself." Speaking for himself, Katz said that talent—not race—determines who plays for the 76ers.

Mike Gminski, who played under Katz and with Barkley as a 76er, may have had the best comment about the whole thing: "It took Charles Barkley to make Dave Hoppen famous. I think Charles is becoming the black Jimmy the Greek."

Management vs. Charles (II)

Of course, his personality is such that Charles does not mesh well with management types at *any* level—coaches and general managers included. About Philly GM Gene Shue, Charles said, "Gene Shue is a clown whose only ambition is to caddie for Harold Katz. He's done nothing to help the situation here. I was good enough to lead us to the championship of the division two years ago before they made all the changes. . . . I have no respect for Gene Shue. He's just a robot."

Then there was the game in 1992 when Barkley missed a wild three-point attempt that possibly cost the Sixers a chance to beat the Chicago Bulls. Philadelphia coach Jim Lynam called the shot "ill-advised," and Barkley jumped all over his case: "I was open, so I took the shot. I do things my way. I've been doing them my way for eight years. If I start worrying about missing shots, then I wouldn't be as good as I am. I missed the shot, but I'm not going to sulk about it all night. Everything I do is wrong," he added, sulking. "It's a no-win situation. If I hit that shot, then everyone would be congratulating me. But if you don't like it, you can kiss my butt or trade me."

Choosing not to take the first option, the Sixers exercised their right to do the latter, trading his butt to Phoenix after that 1992 season. And they left it to new coach Doug Moe (who replaced Lynam) to give the post-mortem on Barkley's last year with the club. "It was disgusting," said Moe. "The bottom line is that he probably wouldn't have played [hard] here. The team was bad last year, he was bad and there was a lot said, and we just didn't think there was any way he would play. I came in thinking he was going to be here, but when you get in, you find out a lot. He had basically quit playing here."

That Old Gang of Mine

Before leaving Philadelphia for Phoenix, Charles made sure to burn as many bridges as he could. Here are a few of his thoughts on his old team and teammates—expressed when he was still on the 76ers:

On how close the 76ers were to an NBA title: "We're close—like Phyllis Diller is close to being Miss America. That's how close we are."

After Atlanta's Kevin Willis outplayed the Sixers' Charles Shackleford at center: "The effort wasn't there. Willis is good, but not that good. Obviously, we've got to get better production from the center spot. That's a no-brainer. I don't mind if someone has a lack of talent. That doesn't bother me. But having a lack of effort isn't fair."

On teammate Hersey Hawkins: "He could score 30 points a night if he wanted to, but for all his talent, he's just not aggressive. He doesn't grab the game by the throat, like he should. If Hersey Hawkins had Andrew Toney's attitude, he'd be illegal."

More on Hawkins, after Hersey criticized Barkley in the press: "I resent that. Two years ago he was an All Star playing with me. I made him a lot better."

How he wasn't going to be Mr. Nice Guy anymore: "We've got a lazy team. If we're not pushed, we don't play. In the past, I would get on a guy's ass and ride them like a horse. But I quit doing that because all the guys complained. Well, you can't worry about feelings when you're below .500. If a guy's not playing well during a game, I'm going to get on his ass like I used to."

On his teammates' attitudes: "We've got so many bitchers and complainers on this team. We've got guys who have complained, complained, and complained. That's why we haven't moved ahead. We don't have total unity. Everybody's got to stick together. We've got a lot of pussies on this team."

More on his teammates' attitudes: "I don't ever want to steal any money from the Sixers. But I've played with guys who need a mask to go pick up their checks."

On what the 76ers needed to do to win: "The team is just bad. Bad team, man. The whole damn team, man. We've got a bad f—— team. Unless we play a perfect game, we can't win. And that's a bad situation. It's really bad when you have to play a perfect game to win."

After an over-the-hill World B. Free was signed by the 76ers in the late eighties: "World B. Free was World B. Off Target."

On Manute Bol: "We traded a first-round draft choice for a 28-year-old flyswatter who could score only 1.9 points per game. Hell, my grandmother could score two points a game as long as she wasn't double-teamed."

During a losing streak by the 76ers: "Where's the strike when you really need it?"

Three Negative Opinions of Charles and His Loud-Mouth Antics

"A great, great player, maybe unstoppable. But he's got no discipline, none. You can't win with a player like that."
—*Phil Jackson*, Chicago Bulls head coach

"I had trouble figuring out his style and adjusting to it. You need a good leader to reach the pinnacle of success. That has yet to come and I don't see any evidence that it will."
    —*Julius Erving*

"If you want stupid comments, Charles Barkley is in Philadelphia."
    —Detroit's *John Salley*, pledging to keep a low profile during a playoff series

Charles Makes Some Jokes Involving His Wife

After being honored as the Philadelphia athlete who had done the most "to reflect credit" on the city, Charles said: "When I first heard about this award, I thought my wife had been doing too much shopping."

On how he views marriage: "Mark Jackson says he loves his fiancée so much he would give up basketball for her. Not me. I love my wife but she can't pay bills like this NBA money can. I'd have to pick [76ers general manager] John Nash over her."

Ever the Patriot, Charles Talks About What It Meant to Represent His Country at the 1992 Olympics

"I'm not a rah rah USA–type guy, so I'm not going to say it would be a great honor to play for the USA. It would be great to go to Spain and have some fun."

While Overseas, Charles Talks About How Much He Misses His Native Land

"I really miss America. I miss hearing if anybody's shot somebody lately."

Charles Goes to Monaco

Before going to Barcelona for the Olympic Games, Charles and his Dream Team cohorts made a stopover in Monaco—a supremely

Julius Erving can criticize Charles Barkley all he wants, but one thing is sure: Charles never had as bad a haircut as Julius did when he was younger. (Photo courtesy of the Philadelphia 76ers)

luxurious little principality next to the French Riviera that, said one writer, "makes Beverly Hills look like Dogpatch." Or as Charles himself put it: "Just like being on spring break in the ghetto."

The Dreams trained hard and practiced hard for a grueling few days in Monaco. Of course, mostly they practiced golf and trained hard at gambling and lounging by the Monte Carlo pools, where some of the women went topless. Charles liked this. "I'm quitting this team for the swim team," he said. "I'm going to the pool as long as there are babes with no tops. You'll think I'm Mark Spitz before this is over."

As befit their royal status, the Dreams were honored guests at a palace dinner hosted by Prince Rainier, the reigning monarch of Monaco. "They say you have to stop eating when he does," Charles noted. "But what if he's having a snack and you're starving? Do you have to eat fast?" Aides to the royal family gave Charles more instructions about etiquette, instructions that reminded him of his former boss, Sixers owner Harold Katz. "They told us you can't touch him and you have to call him 'Your Majesty.' I haven't called anyone 'Your Majesty' since Harold Katz."

What Charles Thought About Whether or Not the Dream Team Should Stay in the Olympic Village

"Do I want to stay in a 100-degree room with three or four roommates? Of course I don't. I think that's a stupid question."

"It's a little unfair to expect us to stay in the Village, because of the magnitude of a Magic Johnson, Michael Jordan, or Larry Bird. We have God on our side, and we're going to stay where God wants us to stay."

"I don't feel like I'm missing any experience by not staying in the Village. Besides, I don't have to. I'm a black millionaire."

What Charles Thought of Dream Team Collegian Christian Laettner

"We're a lot alike actually. We both attended great academic institutions. And when we walk into a room, women scream."

"If I didn't spend time with Chris all he would do is sit in the dark in his room, listening to all the girls screaming for him, and that would be kind of pathetic."

"Hey Christian, we can't find any cards. Run out to 7-Eleven and get us a deck, will you?"
> —Charles to Christian, late one evening during the team's training camp in California

"Christian is going to be the strongest man in the NBA next year, because all he's been doing all summer is carrying around the luggage for 11 guys."
> —during the Olympic tournament

What Oscar Schmidt, the Brazilian Basketball Star, Thought About Playing Against the Dream Team

"I want to play the real Dream Team. They're hiding their game. They have players on the golf course, players with suntans. Why don't they come here to play basketball? I don't care if it's a 100-point difference. I want to see how good they are. I hope they get mad. I hope Charles Barkley gets really mad and plays a little basketball. Not 'Oh, it's a pickup game against Brazil.' I want them to think, 'Let's really beat them bad.' . . . What is this, Bird doesn't play? His back? He'd better get better, because I want to play against him. I'm the same age. I know everything about him. He can't say, 'Oh, my back is hurt.' He has to play."

And What Charles Thought About Playing Against Oscar

"Oscar who? Ain't he the guy on the Odd Couple? I don't know who's gonna guard him. We'll fight each other till the last one's standing, just to have that privilege. Hey, nobody in their right mind wants to play us. But they're from Brazil, and I'm not sure they're in their right mind. They've been sniffin' too much coffee down there. Them and Juan Valdez been havin' too much fun. . . . Oh, I'm so worried. I can't sleep at night, thinkin' about Brazil. I wake up in a cold sweat, thinking, 'Oscar, Oscar.' They're good, they're great. Their vast international experience could hurt us in the long run. Oh, it's lookin' bad."

More Thoughts by Charles on His (and the Dream Team's) Opponents

"We want to send a message to the world. Any team that is going to beat us better bring a lunch bucket and a hard hat."

"All I know about Cuba is they've got some scruffy-looking guy running the country who smokes a cigar."

"Why don't they take their ass-whipping like people and go home?"

Charles Throws an Elbow

Next to spitting on that eight-year-old girl at an NBA game, probably the most disgraceful thing Charles has ever done on a basketball court is throwing that elbow at an Angolan player in the opening game of the Olympic tournament. Bruce Jenkins, who was there, sets the scene:

"Barkley took the court with a vengeance usually reserved for warfare, or a long-standing neighborhood feud. To watch him, you'd think it was a best of seven series and Angola was leading the thing, 3–2. During a perfectly ordinary rebound struggle in the first half, Barkley pushed the rail-thin David Dias, knocking him backward a few feet. Later, during another innocent-looking sequence, he threw a vicious elbow at forward Herlander Coimbra. The Angolans, who have never experienced anything close to world class opposition, seemed a little too awed to take it seriously."

The Angolans may not have taken it seriously, but a lot of other people certainly did, including teammate Michael Jordan. "There just wasn't any place for it," Jordan said. "We were dominating the game. It created mixed feelings, it turned some of the fans against us. There's already some negative feelings about this team. What Charles did just doesn't help." Karl Malone added, "I don't think there's a need to rub anything in someone's face, to degrade someone. We've got a lot of people behind us in this thing. They could turn on us just as fast."

Indeed, many of them did. Barkley was greeted by whistles—the European form of booing—every time he touched the ball, and the people already disgusted with the ugly-American, big-bully image of the Dream Team got even more disgusted. As Larry McShane noted, "Barkley managed to get heckled by people who had never before seen him." But Charles, as is his way, defended his elbow-throwing with a series of statements, all of which had the effect of digging a deeper and deeper hole for himself:

"It's a ghetto thing. He hit me, I hit him. Something you guys [the media] don't understand." (Videotape replays of the game showed no elbowing or rough play by the Angolans prior to Barkley's elbow.)

"The press is so asinine that all they can come up with is my elbow. Here we are at the Olympics and they're making the biggest story my elbow."

"If they gave T's for that in America, I wouldn't make it past the first quarter."

"People told me to hit a fat guy next time, not a skinny one. That guy probably hadn't eaten in a few weeks."

Charles Writes a Column

For the Olympics, Charles got together with *USA Today* to write a column about the Dream Team and their march to a gold medal. But it's against the rules for an Olympic athlete to write such a column, unless it's for his or her hometown paper. So the USOC told Charles to cut it out.

Said an irritated Barkley: "The USOC is a little jealous of our success. It's an ego thing. We don't think we're above the Olympic Committee, but it shouldn't pick on every little thing we do. We should be given our due for being a great basketball team."

Responded Mike Moran of the U.S. Olympic Committee: "The

Dream Team is out of touch with the rest of the Olympic team. They must abide by the rules like any other U.S. athlete. The IOC is asking us to enforce their rule. We're simply complying with the IOC request. To say we're jealous shows Barkley is extremely out of touch with what we're doing here."

Out of touch or no, Barkley's musings continued to appear in *USA Today* for the rest of the games. Only they appeared under the byline of sportswriter David DuPre, and Barkley's name was left off.

The Great Sweats Brouhaha

A far greater controversy at the Games hinged on this question: Would Charles Barkley, Michael Jordan, and others under contract to Nike wear the Reebok-made warm-up suits on the awards stand after the Dream Team's inevitable gold medal? Since there was no suspense about whether or not the Dream Team would win their games—it was just a question of how much they would win by—the hordes of media had to write and talk about *something*. This was that something.

The rules were that all U.S. Olympic team members had to wear the Reebok apparel on the medal stand. Reebok had paid a lot of money to the USOC for this privilege, and it applied to all athletes. But Reebok is a bitter competitor of Nike's, and Jordan and Barkley, out of loyalty to *their* shoe firm, said no, causing more headaches for the overwhelmed Mike Moran. "They may be your Dream Team," said the USOC spokesman, "but they're my nightmare."

In characteristic fashion, Charles made sure to throw gas on the flames with typically incendiary remarks: "Us Nike guys are loyal to Nike because they pay us a lot of money," he said. "I have two million reasons not to wear Reebok." As if anybody needed to be reminded how much the Dream Teamers make. And then when somebody informed Charles that the USOC would not allow him or any of the others to accept their medals if they weren't wearing their Reeboks, Charles said, "Well, they are going to have to get their butts waxed. They'd better bring some big guys."

But if anybody got their butts waxed, it was probably Nike (which got a ton of negative publicity, despite saying that it had told their players they could wear the Reebok stuff) and the Dream Teamers,

Charles Barkley can keep talkin' and squawkin', as long as he keeps jammin' and slammin'. (Photo by Mike Maicher)

particularly Barkley and Jordan. "I feel very strongly about loyalty to my own company," said Jordan, a comment that invited ridicule from columnist Mike Littwin: "I'm waiting for him to say he regrets he has but one life to give to his shoe company."

Jordan and Barkley ended up wearing the Reebok gear (using the American flag draped around their shoulders to cover the logo), but Scott Ostler had the inside scoop on what Michael really wanted to do at the Olympics: "Jordan, I hear, really wanted to take part in the opening ceremonies but backed out when the USOC denied him permission to wear a huge Nike shoe on his head."

Dream Team Backlash

Maybe it was the Great Sweats Brouhaha, or all the things that Charles said and did, or the lopsided nature of the games. Or maybe it was just . . . *the whole thing.* In any case, some people did not express unbridled joy at the sight of Charles, Michael, Magic, and the rest of the Dream Teamers wreaking basketball havoc on the world. One of those people was Mike Barrowman, a gold medal–winning swimmer for the United States. "There are two Olympics, two different things going on here," he said at the time. "One is the Olympics and one is basketball. It's like we're seeing the NBA take precedence over the Olympics. It doesn't make much sense to the American athletes." He added sardonically, in a reference to the high-living ways of the Dream Team millionaires, "They're staying in the nicest hotel in Barcelona. They're flying helicopters into the games. Just like the Hungarians, huh?"

The Dream Team backlash became so pronounced in certain quarters that a few party-poopers in the media began hoping for the impossible—an upset of the big, bad Americans. "I want to be there when the music stops for American basketball," wrote Leigh Montville. "I want to laugh a little bit as windbag predictions by glib authorities are flattened. Is this unpatriotic? I think not. The U.S. basketball team, built with such pretentious glee and such outrageous expectations, has become the ultimate bully."

San Francisco columnist Joan Ryan agreed. "When the U.S. wins the gold medal, it will be as exciting as a whistle blowing to end a factory shift. The work is done. Time to go home. The gold medal goes up on the mantle with the MVP trophy, the NBA championship trophy, the NCAA championship trophy." She added longingly, "I want to see a team fall to the floor in tears. I want to see a moment that makes somebody's life. I want to hear about parades in the streets of the capital city. I want what the Olympics offer at their best: a real dream team."

Charles Responds to the Anti–Dream Team Faction

"This is all I hear, bitching and complaining. When we lost the Olympics [in 1988], you bitched and complained. If we win here, you'll bitch and complain. I don't know about what, but you'll find something. Down in the Olympic Village, they're complaining. I hear the swimmers and track people are upset we're not staying down there. Did they ever stop to think that we've got Magic Johnson and Michael Jordan on this team? It wouldn't be the same for those athletes if we went down there. People would be all over us. It would be disruptive. Hell, they don't even have beds that fit us in that place."

"Everybody's complaining about pros in the Olympics. Why don't I hear anything about Steffi Graf or Jim Courier being here? Aren't they professionals? Don't they make millions of dollars? Are you telling me the track people aren't pros? I don't want to hear any shit out of them. The way I see it, a lot of people want to see us prove we're the best basketball players in the world. If other people don't like it, they can turn the fucking television off."

Charles Talks More About His Friends in the Media

"I never realized you could get so many ugly guys together at the same time."

> —while being interviewed by dozens of reporters at the 1990 All Star Game

"There is no MVP. There are just a lot of great players. Are you going to tell me that Ewing is better than Jordan, or is Jordan bet-

ter than Magic? It's a stupid vote by a bunch of people who have no clue."
—on the 1990 MVP race

"The American media, they're a bunch of nitwits anyway."
—at the 1992 Olympics

And the Media Talks About Charles

"Somewhere along the line, the 'colorful' Charles Barkley has become the 'unbearable' Charles Barkley. There used to be a sense of anticipation whenever his name was mentioned, a chuckle at news of his latest contretemps. Which Philadelphia 76er teammate did he openly ridicule this time? What was it he said about Sixer owner Harold Katz? How blue were his comments to fans who were riding him? Now it's different. The newswire carrying the Barkley Chronicles is still clack-clack-clacking away, but there are fewer and fewer interested readers. They've reached the saturation point. . . . Lower the decibel level. Charles, get your act together off the court, and play ball with your teammates."
—*Jack McCallum*

"Sir Charles's mouth runs like a refrigerator—non-stop. . . . When it comes to the Dream Team, Barkley is that loud noise interrupting your REM sleep."
—*Larry McShane*

"He's a dope. He has to be. Nobody behaves like that who is not a dope."
—*Joan Ryan*

"I think Charles wants to see if he can leave the Olympics with an IQ lower than his uniform number. He went to Barcelona as a refreshingly candid, if occasionally boorish, kind of guy, and he has degenerated into a babbling buffoon. The Dream Teamers keep saying they're on a mission. [Barkley's] mission is to offend, embarrass and repulse Americans of every race, creed and color."
—*Scott Ostler*

And Finally, What Charles Thinks of the People Who Ultimately Pay His Salary, the People in the Seats

"Kids are great. That's one of the best things about our business, all the kids you get to meet. It's a shame they have to grow up to be regular people and come to the games and call you names."

"My dream is for a fan to come at me in an alley and grab me— and be pounded through the concrete."

March Madness:
A Look at the College Game

College basketball has blossomed in recent years, especially with the boom in popularity of "March Madness." The NCAA basketball tournament has become one of the most exciting and colorful sporting events anywhere. Here's a look at some of the coaches, players, and teams that have helped make March so darned mad.

Mobsters of Basketball, or Just Misunderstood?

With Larry Johnson and Stacey Augmon as their stars, the 1990 national championship Running Rebels of the University of Nevada at Las Vegas were a supremely talented group, but they also carried with them a reputation for thuggery on the court. "They play like thugs," said broadcaster Barry Tompkins, in remarks he later denied making. "They have a lot of guys you wouldn't want to bring home unless everything is bolted down."

Although Tompkins ate his words, others said much the same thing. "All you have to know about the Running Rebels is that if Saddam Hussein could bury the 'three,' " Phil Jackman joked, "there's a good chance he'd be in their backcourt." And Loyola Marymount's Chris Knight explained what it was like to play against the taunting UNLV squad: "Other teams, like a Michigan, will yell: 'Where's your jump shot?' But Vegas will yell: 'Where's your mother? I think she's in my room.' "

The trash-talking came to an ugly culmination in a hotly contested regional clash between UNLV and Ball State, which was narrowly won by the Rebels. After the game Moses Scurry openly mocked Ball State coach Dick Hunsaker, who reacted heatedly,

Before signing with Charlotte of the NBA, Larry Johnson played for the gangsters of college basketball, the Runnin' Rebs of UNLV. (Photo by Brad Mangin)

calling UNLV "a disgrace to basketball. . . . Those guys are a bunch of thugs and you can quote me."

Jerry Tarkanian always stood up for his players and said that they were the best group of guys he'd ever coached. When he heard Hunsaker's comments, he responded with his own heat: "He's a complete idiot," said Tarkanian. "He took over a 29–3 team from Rick Majerus that had all five starters back plus Charles Thompson, and he brought them in at 26–6. What he should do is figure out what the hell he did wrong and keep his mouth shut."

Take Duke—and 31 Points

Thugs or no, those Runnin' Rebs could play some ball. And in winning the 1990 national title they thumped the Goody Two Shoes contingent from Duke, 103–73. While awed by the men from Vegas in the championship game, columnist Allan Malamud was not so impressed with Duke's performance. "Duke couldn't even execute the high five properly," he said.

Following that loss, Duke coach Mike Krzyzewski had to endure a long and painful off-season filled with jokes at his expense. One jokester was Jim Valvano, the former North Carolina State coach, who, at a banquet honoring Coach K., told the audience, "You know, Mike had a tough summer, having to live with that loss. But I just want Mike to know I was with him all the way. I knew he'd get it done. I had Duke and 31."

Blood Feud

One of the nastiest feuds ever between a basketball coach and his university—and there have been a few—occurred between Jerry Tarkanian and the University of Nevada at Las Vegas after the Runnin' Rebels won the 1990 NCAA title. Tarkanian argued publicly and heatedly with UNLV president Robert Maxson and other school officials over his basketball program. Although Tark the Shark had turned the little-known desert school into a national basketball powerhouse, his program was beseiged by charges of recruiting irregularities, gambling, point shaving by players; there were NCAA and even FBI investigations, and other problems. It was one of those ugly situations in which everyone gets hurt, and nobody wins. Here are some of the things that were said during the fight.

"I'm embarrassed and I'm tired, but I think this university's at a crossroads. And I believe the nation is watching UNLV to see if we're going to be a serious academic institution or a basketball team with a university attached. Jerry has said that if I had cooperated with him I could have been governor of this state. Well, I don't want to be governor. I want to be president of a good university."

—*Robert Maxson*

"We've always withstood other people taking shots at us. But the bad thing is when you find out your own people are doing it to you. That's just mind-boggling."

—*Jerry Tarkanian*

"We got torn up from the inside. We got dismantled from the inside. It's totally unbelievable."

—*Jerry Tarkanian*

"Maxson's a rookie at the president's game. The out-of-state enrollment here is wholly the result of basketball success. The schools he wants to compete with have alumni who have CEOs and in the White House, and he thinks he's gonna get the crème de la crème? This university's a baby. If you're the crème de la crème, you don't send your child to a town where prostitution is practically legal. That's what kills me about Maxson. He's got a marketing tool, and he wants to eliminate it."

—*Elmore Spencer*, who played at UNLV under Tarkanian

"I'm angry and I've had my fill of ridiculous charges against my administration by people who really don't care about this university and who will stoop to any level to avoid accepting responsibility for the messes made here which others are now trying to clean up."

—*Robert Maxson*

"This hurts so much. To be defamed and have this shadow cast upon them [his players] is the lowest thing I've ever heard of. It's unforgivable, just unforgivable."
> —*Jerry Tarkanian*, about rumors of possible point shaving by his players

"I think anytime a person can't or won't accept responsibility for his own circumstances, he looks to blame others. That's true in his case."
> —*Sheila Strike-Bolla,* the wife of UNLV's women's basketball coach (Strike-Bolla reportedly was involved in videotaping [from an air duct in the gymnasium] an alleged "illegal" practice by Tarkanian's team)

"I think Sheila Strike sharpened the blade on me."
> —*Jerry Tarkanian*, joking after cutting his hand while peeling an apple (not joking, Tarkanian has also called Strike-Bolla "a snake")

"This humiliation that even an investigation will cause this university, its faculty, staff, and thousands of students can't be overstated. For anyone to say or imply that we would encourage publicity by leaking such news reflects stupidity beyond imagination. I categorically deny such mindless charges, though I shouldn't have to."
> —*Robert Maxson,* responding to reports that his administration leaked news of an NCAA investigation into violations by the UNLV basketball program

"F—— the school!"
> —the chant the UNLV players used when they broke their huddle after a timeout (some students also wore T-shirts that said KEEP TARK on the front side and FIRE MAXSON on the back)

"I think the community is fed up with the whole situation. It's tired of the constant battles with the NCAA. It's tired of the battles between the university and basketball program. And it's tired

of the enormous money poured into a dark hole to defend basketball with so little positive return."
     —*Sheila Strike-Bolla*

"In my wildest dreams I never thought this would take place. [Tarkanian] built more than a basketball program. This is a known school. They can say what they want to, but he's built more than they ever realized."
     —*Tim Grgurich*, Tarkanian's assistant coach

"Not one violation relates to any of the coaches. Most of them are Mickey Mouse. There's not a program at UNLV that could be put through four and a half years of an investigation by their own university and not come up with a single major violation."
     —*Jerry Tarkanian*

"They've tried to tear something out of the man who's been good to the game and good to the kids in the game. It's embarrassing to the game what this school has done. They're embarrassing the game of basketball. They're embarrassing the coaching profession."
     —*Tim Grgurich*

"Something is wrong when you lose humanism in an institution of higher education."
     —*Lois Tarkanian*, Jerry's wife

"I'd like to be able to go to practice and then go have a beer with Rollie. But we can't, because if he said anything in support of [UNLV president Robert] Maxson, I'd vomit."
     —*Jerry Tarkanian*, when asked how he was getting along with the man hired to replace him, Rollie Massimino

Mike Lupica, on Christian Laettner

He was one of the most storied players in college basketball history, and the only collegian to play on the Dream Team. The 1991–92 College Player of the Year, he was an All-American center who led Duke to back-to-back NCAA titles in 1991 (over UNLV) and 1992 (over Michigan). So what does New York columnist Mike Lupica have against Christian Laettner? Let him tell you:

"Despite shooting ten for ten from the field and ten for ten from the line against Kentucky in the finals of the [1992] East Regional, and making one of the most memorable pressure shots in college basketball history to finally win the game for Duke, Laettner will be remembered as much for stomping on the chest of a Kentucky kid named Aminu Timberlake. If they ever make a movie of Christian Laettner's life, they ought to call it *White Man Can Jump but Only on a Little-Known Sub Who's Flat on His Back.*"

Lupica continues, "Believe me, it wasn't the only time Laettner did something like this at Duke during his matinee idol career. It was just the time he got caught with all the lights on. It's a good thing he got his cheap shots in while still safely in college because he's about to go into the pros and become the most overrated Duke graduate since, oh, Danny Ferry. I want to be at the NBA game when Laettner tries to do the Durham Stomp against Karl 'The Mailman' Malone."

If truth be known, it isn't just Laettner that Mike Lupica dislikes; he just doesn't like the whole Duke thing.

"I mean, is there a group of athletes anywhere else in the world more precious than the Judd Nelsons of college basketball?" he wrote on another occasion. "If you were wondering what happened to Mr. Chips's kids, now you know. . . . I like Bobby Hurley when he isn't whining to the refs. And you have to respect Mike Krzyzewski's record, even though he once convened a meeting of student sportswriters and proceeded to evaluate their work with language most often reserved for referees. Bob Knight pulls a stunt like that, and he's doing time with Michael Milken. But Coach K.— he gets away with it."

And, returning to his favorite subject, Lupica added, "And how about Christian Laettner? Now there's a fun kid. He was once described as the center for the Dead Poets Society, smug and aloof. Funny, I don't remember anybody from Dead Poets U. ever elbowing an opponent upside the head."

More About Christian's Stomp

Despite his coverboy looks and choirboy image, Christian Laettner could talk trash and throw elbows with the best of them, as Mike Lupica points out. There was that 1991 NCAA tournament game in which Laettner's trash-talking pissed off Connecticut's Brad Sellers so much that he tried to push Christian's pretty head through the gym floor. "I just wanted to kill him," said Sellers afterward. "In fact I still do. If I saw him now I would try to hurt him." Earlier in that same tournament Laettner showed up Iowa's Acie Earl by laughing in his face after being called for a foul. Coach K. told his center to knock it off.

But the worst moment of Laettner's college career was easily the stomping episode in that classic game against Kentucky. It was a blatant act witnessed by millions on TV and by his mother, Bonnie Laettner, who was wearing a neck brace following surgery. "Did you see Laettner's mother on TV?" one radio announcer cracked after the game. "He must have stepped on her neck."

Chuck Person Gives His Views on the Stomp

Sharpshooting pro forward Chuck Person, however, has a more charitable view of Christian's stomp. When Person joined number-one draft pick Laettner on the Minnesota Timberwolves in 1992, Chuck said he had never seen his new teammate play in college. "But I understand he stepped on a guy's chest," said Chuck. "That's right down my alley. I can relate to a guy like that."

Two Early Assessments of Christian Laettner as a Pro

"I think he'll eventually have the credentials to back up everything he thinks of himself."
—*Jack McCloskey*, Timberwolves general manager

"I've talked to Christian an awful lot this season. He's got an aw-

ful lot of pride, and sometimes he can be stubborn. But he's got a heart, I think."
—*Chuck Person*

Trash-Talking

The pros do it, the college boys do it, even the preps do it. Hell, the kids playing CYO ball may be doing it these days. It comes from the streets, and it's called trash-talking. The object is to throw your opponent off his game and maybe even humiliate him by jawing at him and riding him verbally after you've made a good play against him. "Talking trash," says broadcaster and former Marquette star George Thompson, "is definitely an art form." And while players on every level of basketball may talk smack, the college guys have perfected it. Here are some recent examples of the art form from the colleges:

"Sorry, man. Thought it was the ball. Couldn't tell the difference."
—Wyoming's *Travis Butler*, after grabbing the head of Louisville guard Everick Sullivan during a fight for a loose ball

"Elevator's going to nine, baby. I'm dropping you off at six!"
—a typical expression as a player scores over another (after a dunk, a player might yell in the face of the poor sap trying to defend him, "Flight school!")

"I'm gonna take you to the hoop, then I'm takin' your mom."
—a line often used by guard *Todd Day* when he played for Arkansas

"I flushed on you!"
—*Khari Jaxon* of New Mexico, after dunking on an opposing player

"Yo, Toine. We're coming to Ann Arbor in a couple of weeks. Lose 10."
—*Scott Skiles*, then with Michigan State, ragging on the overweight Michigan guard Antoine Joubert

"If you're such a good defensive coach, why don't you get somebody out here to stop me?"

> —*Scott Skiles* to Georgetown's John Thompson, when Skiles was running wild offensively in a game against the Hoyas some years ago

"I don't care how good you play. I'm still the number-one draft choice."

> —*Shaquille O'Neal* to Arizona's Sean Rooks, after Rooks badly outplayed O'Neal in a game in his senior year at LSU

"I thought you were 6'7", but you're just a little fella. You shouldn't be playin' inside. Why don't you bring your little self out here where you belong?"

> —Michigan guard and supreme trash-talker *Jalen Rose*, telling Oklahoma State forward Byron Houston to come out to the backcourt with him

"It doesn't matter, you're still gonna lose."

> —*Jalen Rose* to a Cincinnati player, after the Bearcats took a temporary lead in their 1992 Final Four game (Rose was right; the Bearcats lost)

"I wasn't on the committee."

> —Michigan's *Jimmy King*, when asked what he thought of Duke's Bobby Hurley being named 1992 Final Four MVP (King also described Hurley's play as "average")

"I don't really feel bad for them, to tell you the truth. I didn't talk trash before the game, those guys did. You just have to have a little respect."

> —*Bobby Hurley*, after his Duke squad clobbered Michigan to win the 1992 championship (Hurley wore a T-shirt that said, YOU CAN TALK THE GAME. BUT CAN YOU PLAY THE GAME?)

"There's a difference between confidence and arrogance. That's

Former Kentucky star Rex Chapman could talk some pretty good smack himself when he was in college. Playing against Louisville center Felton Spencer, he'd come down the court and yell out, "Hey Felton, this jumper's for you," just before canning an outside shot. (Photo courtesy of the Charlotte Hornets)

the stuff that bites you in the butt, right there. They talked a lot of trash before the game. We get to talk it after. Now they just look foolish."

> —Duke center *Cherokee Parks*, after Duke again whipped Michigan in a rematch the next season following their 1992 title game

"Let me get your names. You need to be on the roll sheet, 'cause school's in session."

> —*Michael Jordan* to a group of college players he was about to play against in a pickup game

Duke's Greatest Jeers

Duke University students are renowned for their rowdy, insulting behavior at basketball games. But the Cameron Indoor Stadium crazies are not just rude and obnoxious, they're clever and funny too. A few of their highlights and lowlights:

• At the 1992 Final Four, the Duke cheering section chanted "Chair . . . chair. . . . chair" at Indiana coach Bobby Knight, referring to the time he threw one across the court during a game.

• In the 1990 NCAA Finals against basketball-tough but academically suspect Nevada–Las Vegas, the Blue Devil mascot paraded around courtside with a sign that read, WELCOME FELLOW SCHOLARS.

• Upon seeing North Carolina coach Jim Valvano enter Cameron arena, the Dukies yelled "Sit! Sit! Sit!" When Valvano, always ready to engage and entertain, promptly sat down on the court, they began yelling, "Roll over! Roll over!"

• Duke has traditionally been very hard on nearby rival NC State, particularly when Valvano was coach and the Wolfpack was mired in recruiting controversies and scandal. At a game during this period, the Dukies pointed to Duke coach Mike Krzyzewski and chanted, "Good coach, good coach," then turned to Valvano and chanted, "Bad coach, bad coach . . . "

• After it was revealed that members of the NC State basketball team had profited from under-the-table shoe deals, the Duke fans bombarded the floor with dozens of pairs of sneakers when the Wolfpack came to Cameron Indoor Stadium.

• A Duke chant: "If you can't go to college, go to State. / If you can't go to State, go to jail."

• NC State players get no mercy from the Dukies. Caught stealing aspirin from a North Carolina pharmacy in the 1970s, Moe Rivers got a headache from all the aspirin that was thrown at him at Cameron. The Wolfpack's Lorenzo Charles was charged with stealing pizzas from a deliveryman; the Dukies bombarded *him* with empty pizza boxes. Then there was the North Carolina State star who owned two luxury automobiles. His torture? Duke fans waved car keys from the stands and jangled them at him.

• The merry pranksters of Duke play no favorites. If you're an opposing player and you have a weakness to exploit, they'll make fun of it. Georgia Tech's Dennis Scott lost 30 pounds in the off-season but was subjected to a shower of donuts, pastries, Twinkies, and bagels when he was introduced before a game at Duke.

• When North Carolina's Steve Hale experienced breathing problems during a game, one side of the ever-helpful Duke rooting section chanted, "*In*-hale," while the other side answered "*Ex*-hale."

• Sometimes the Dukies go too far. In 1984, after a University of Maryland starter was charged with sexually assaulting a woman, they spelled out R-A-P-E in the stands and threw condoms at him. Criticized for this display, Duke made up for it the next game by giving two dozen roses to North Carolina coach Dean Smith, saying "We beg to differ" instead of "Bullshit!" at calls by referees, and waving PLEASE MISS signs when Tarheel players were shooting free throws.

• Eric Montross, North Carolina's seven-foot-tall center, was a target of the Dukesters. During the 1992 season, they produced a parody of North Carolina's student paper, *The Daily Tar Hole,* with a large blank space on the front page. The caption underneath the space read, "This big useless white space was placed here to remind you of Eric Montross."

• One of the cleverest-ever jibes came years ago when Maryland featured a fine 6'9" center named Tom Roy. Roy always seemed to play his best games against Duke, and when he came to Cameron to play he was greeted by signs that said, TOM ROY SUCKS! The year after Roy graduated, Maryland returned to Cameron only to see signs saying, TOM ROY STILL SUCKS!

Going Overboard

Sometimes college students can go a bit overboard in their zeal to root their schools on to victory. One thinks of the merciless hazing that Patrick Ewing endured while he was playing for Georgetown. Students at other schools made fun of his supposed lack of intelligence—EWING KAN'T READ DIS was one banner, while at Seton Hall they held up signs that said THINK! EWING! THINK!— and there were racial euphemisms as well.

Steve Kerr knows about nastiness, too. Kerr was a brilliant shooting and playmaking guard for Arizona whose father, Malcom Kerr, was murdered in 1984 by two Arab terrorists while he was serving as president of the American University in Beirut. Kerr was then a freshman at Arizona, and four years later he and Sean Elliott would lead the Wildcats to the NCAA Final Four. Such a family tragedy did not immunize Kerr from the jerks in the stands, however. In his senior year, preparing to play cross-state rival Arizona State, a small group of ASU fans began a chant directed at him: "PLO, PLO! Hey, Kerry, where's your dad?" they chanted, adding, "PLO, PLO! Go back to Beirut!"

Ladies and gentlemen, that is the very definition of bad taste, and Kerr was so stunned by it that he could not reply.

Steve Responds to Cal

Fortunately, the heckling that Kerr received in other places at other times was somewhat more good-natured. One school that gave him a particularly bad time was Cal–Berkeley. After every home game at Harmon Gym, Cal students would name a visiting player as "Tuna of the Game." Kerr had been the Tuna so often and been the butt of so many jokes that the editor of Cal's student newspaper, in a gesture of goodwill, gave Kerr a chance to write a column in the *Daily Californian* and respond to all the years of abuse he'd received. This was Kerr's message to his longtime tormentors at Cal:

"Well, Cal fans, the roles are reversed. The shoe is on the other foot. After four years of taking more abuse from you than Larry Holmes's face took from Mike Tyson's fist, I finally get my chance to get back. At last I can throw insults your way, fully aware that you will see them, read them, and know them. Yes, Cal fans, the Tuna is on the other sandwich.

"I'd like to take this time to respond to some of the more prominent insults I've heard during my career. First to the guy in the referee shirt in the front row who mockingly shouted, 'How's the knee?!' for two hours straight last year, I say, 'It's doing quite well, thank you. How's your brain?'

"To the earthy-looking, Birkenstock-wearing girl who, during one game two years ago, repeatedly yelled, 'Kerr, what kind of hair spray do you use?' I say, 'Before you and all the rest of Berkeley ask for advice on hair spray, try thinking about the simple basics of personal hygiene—like showering.' Also, to the Shakey's employees who double as Cal band members, and who each year obnoxiously parade across the floor as we attempt to warm up, I ask, 'Why don't you stay off of Pete Newell Court? You're an embarrassment to Harmon Gym—not to mention Harmon Arena. Or is it Newell Pavilion? Or the Harmon Alameda Coliseum? Or . . . the Granola Dome?'

"Finally, to all of you sophisticated intellectuals who each year cleverly ask, 'Hey Kerr, why don't you go to a *real* school?' I say, 'I wanted to, but Stanford didn't accept my application.'"

And While We're on the Subject, What About Those Stanford Students Anyway?

"You might expect Stanford fans to pack Maples Pavilion on Thursday and Saturday nights for the final two home games of the season. And they might—if someone would give them directions to the gym. Yes sir, Maples will be rockin'—unless there's a sale on hooded sweatshirts at the bookstore. Or a new bike trail map coming out. At Stanford, when you say you're looking for someone to lead 'Cheers' on Thursday night, they think you mean Ted Danson."

—*C. W. Nevius*, commenting on the apathetic Stanford crowds

The College Beat

Random jokes, observations, caustic comments, and other odds and ends from the college game of recent years:

"Hey, Bobby Hurley's gonna make my All–Bill Laimbeer team! A whiner, a moaner, and a groaner. I mean, come on, Bobby!"
> —*Dick Vitale*, moaning about a Bobby Hurley pout after a call went against his Duke team

"Duke has at least matched what Wooden and UCLA did in their dynasty years. Look it up. UCLA did it against claimers. Duke did it in the Breeders' Cup."
> —*Mark Whicker*, after Duke's second straight national title in 1992, noting that its winning percentage in the NCAA tournament matched that of John Wooden's at UCLA

"To lose to a team like this, in our own gym, is a joke. And there's no way that should happen. On their best day, they shouldn't be able to beat us."
> —UCLA senior *Don MacLean*, after crosstown rival USC beat the Bruins in their first meeting during the 1991–92 season (the two teams met again later in the season and USC won that one, too)

"I'm disappointed. I've always wanted to play against a Bob Knight team. Kansas has good talent—I'm not going to downgrade any team or any coach—but I wanted to go out there and brutally beat Indiana with Arkansas-style ball."
> —Arkansas center *Oliver Miller*, expressing disappointment that the Razorbacks would play Kansas— not Indiana—in the 1991 NCAA regional championships

"I think about what he said, and it still gets me mad. They're dis-

appointed they didn't get to play Indiana? Guess they're real disappointed now."
> —Kansas forward *Olonzo Jamison*, after Kansas whipped Arkansas on its way to the NCAA title

"You want to know the theory people play with today? Coaches tell their kids, 'All five of you guys go ahead and foul at once, because they can only call one of 'em.' "
> —*Sonny Smith*, Virginia Commonwealth coach

"Byron Houston had four takedowns and two reversals. Don't those count for two points each?"
> —Missouri coach *Norm Stewart*, after being mugged in a game by Houston and Oklahoma State

"At Princeton when they go to dunk, they say 'Please' before they go to the hoop."
> —*Darryl Dawkins*

"Coach P. J. Carlesimo is one of our favorites, but at times his Seton Hall team performs as if the players had been introduced to each other just moments before tipoff."
> —*Gene Wojciechowski*, sportswriter, during the 1992 season

"In Oklahoma, if you can't sleep, the doctor gives you a prescription to watch a Big East basketball game."
> —Oklahoma coach *Billy Tubbs*

"What I meant to say was that on videotapes of Big East games, they have a disclaimer that says: 'Caution. May Cause Drowsiness.' "
> —*Billy Tubbs*, clarifying his statement on the Big East

"Is Lute on something?"
> —USC coach *George Raveling*, after Arizona's Lute Olson said it was harder to win a road game at Cal or Stanford than at Duke

"Cal's basketball team netted 'one of the best recruiting classes' ever this year. Haven't we heard that before? Oh yeah, in 1990, 1989, 1988, 1987 . . . "
—*Henry Schulman*, critic

IF YOU WENT TO THE BATHROOM, YOU PROBABLY MISSED HIM.
—newspaper headline about Cal freshman John Carty, who fouled out after only five minutes of play in his first-ever game in 1988

"Pepperdine isn't a college basketball team, it's a toothpaste."
—joke about the Malibu college

"When he arrived at UNLV, he was 6'4" and 139 pounds. He looked like he was built out of swizzle sticks. Now, of course, he's much bigger. Last year, he measured 6'5" and weighed 152. He looks like he's built out of bread sticks."
—*C. W. Nevius*, on former UNLV player Travis Bice

"If we're number 17 in the nation, it's a sick nation."
—*Wimp Sanderson*, after learning that one 1992 pre-season poll ranked his Alabama team in the top 20 in the country

"He's accusing the whole league of being racist. But he'll have to substantiate his charges. I realize this has been a very tough year for Washington and his program. His program is really the pits."
—Missouri Valley Conference Commissioner *Doug Elgin,* responding to charges by Drake coach Rudy Washington that he had been subjected to racial slurs while playing road games in the MVC in 1991

"Let me tell you, gang. San Francisco, Seattle, and Los Angeles are a hell of a lot better than Champaign, West Lafayette, and Bloomington and all those other horsefeather towns."
—Arizona State coach *Bill Frieder*, commenting on the

difference between coaching in the Pac-10 versus the Big Ten (where he was head man for Michigan)

"He got tired of his dad writing him for money."
—broadcaster *Beano Cook*, on why a star basketball player dropped out of college

Big John's Olympic Disaster

John Thompson has coached one NCAA championship team at Georgetown, but clearly his greatest coaching disaster was the 1988 Olympics. Some people will never forget how he left players like Sean Elliott off the team, or how he kept only one good outside shooter (Hersey Hawkins) while choosing two point guards (Charles Smith, Bimbo Coles) who were good defensive players but hardly represented the best the U.S. had to offer at that position. Mostly, his critics can't forget how that team *lost*—the only U.S. men's team to lose a fair-and-square basketball game in Olympic history. (The 1972 U.S. squad, the victim of the biggest rip-off in Olympic history, does not count, say the critics.)

David Robinson, who played center on that team and tried to conform to Thompson's rigid coaching schemes, can't forget 1988 either. "Thompson was a dictator," Robinson told a magazine interviewer after the games were over. "You had to go his way. It was always his gym, his team, his this. . . . He wants you scared of him. He degrades you. He told me I couldn't play. I said, 'Okay, that's fine, I can't play.' He didn't understand how I could be devoted to the game and still have other interests. He was used to having kids for whom basketball is everything. He gets into your mentality. I just didn't agree with the mind games he plays."

In his reply to Robinson, Thompson said, "All I say is it wasn't his role to disagree with me. I don't permit people to question me, or else they're not on my team." Thompson's autocratic methods played havoc with the minds of other Olympic players too. "Every player has gone through the state where he felt 'I'm going to get cut,' " said Charles Smith. "He doesn't tell you what he wants. He tells you what he wants as a team, but not individually. That gets confusing."

After scrimmaging against the U.S. Olympians prior to the games in Seoul, Seattle center Alton Lister said, "He doesn't look like he knows exactly what they're trying to accomplish out there." Lister was talking about David Robinson, but he could have been talking about Smith and the rest of the team as well.

The Americans were beaten in the semifinals by a fine Russian team that starred Sarunas Marciulionis, now a guard with the Golden State Warriors. The loss proved so embarrassing that it provided the impetus for NBA stars to represent the United States in the next Olympics. Many onlookers blamed the defeat on the improved international game and the fact that the Russians trained and played together as a unit year-round. But others pointed at Thompson, and they found an unlikely supporter for their view in the coach of that Russian squad, Alexander Gomelski.

"Thompson is good coach and this is a very nice team that he has," Gomelski explained in his halting English to the *Los Angeles Times*. "People do not believe it possible that we won—only me. [Before the game with the United States] even the best Russian players are saying we are never going to cross the center line. The Americans have a very good press defense . . . it is a good Thompson press defense. But," Gomelski went on, "Thompson had an idea in his mind on how the game was going to go, based on what happened in games before that. He didn't want to change this. He went straight ahead without adjusting. The coach has to feel how the game goes. That's what coaching is all about."

Lefty

In a 1980 game between Georgetown and Maryland, an irate John Thompson called Terrapins coach Lefty Driesell "a motherfucker." Thompson later expressed regret for the comment, and Driesell was asked if he accepted the apology. "Of course I do," said Lefty. "To err is human, to forgive is divine, and I'm divine."

Well, Lefty was hardly that. Though he coached some fine teams at Maryland, he resigned in disgrace following the Len Bias cocaine overdose tragedy. And a lot of people were happy about that because they thought his coaching methods and recruiting techniques were unscrupulous.

Nevertheless, Lefty had a nice, folksy wit that made people laugh. After one of his players tossed up an air ball in a scrimmage, the bald-headed coach took him aside and said, "Jerry, if you keep taking shots like that, Coach Ellis [an assistant coach] is gonna pull out all his hair and end up lookin' like me."

More bald jokes were supplied by his friends. Terry Holland, who used to play for Driesell and went on to become a coach in his own right, tells what it was like to go on recruiting trips with Driesell: "When Lefty Driesell used to go recruiting out in the boonies, he'd roll the window of his car down and get arrested for mooning." And Bill Foster summed up Lefty's career perfectly: "I once talked with Lefty's parents. His mother wanted him to be a doctor and his father wanted him to be a basketball coach. They both were disappointed."

The Dark Knight of Indiana

I f Bobby Knight were in baseball, he'd be George Steinbrenner. If he were a Middle Eastern despot, he'd be Saddam Hussein. Or Qaddafi. Flip a coin. If he had lived centuries ago and hung out with the Huns, he would've been Attila. If he was a member of the shark family, he'd be a Great White. If he were a dinosaur, he'd be a tyrannosaurus. If he was a horror movie character, he'd be Freddy. Or maybe the guy in the hockey mask.

Of course, Bobby Knight is not any of these things; he is the basketball coach for Indiana University. The man who threw a chair across the court while a game was in progress. The coach of three national titles and a gold medal–winning Olympic team. The man who pulled his team off the floor in a game against the Russians and who has caused more international incidents than Arafat. The man who pretended to lash one of his black Indiana players with a bullwhip.

Ladies and gentlemen, the tyrannical, the lordly, the occasionally amusing, the sometimes admirable, the often despicable, the manipulative, the delusional, the manic, the raging bull of Bloomington, Mr. Bobby Knight!

Bobby Goes Bananas

The definitive work on Bobby Knight is *A Season on the Brink,* John Feinstein's fascinating and disturbing look at what it is like to play basketball for Indiana University under Knight. Feinstein had access to him like no reporter before or since, and so he was able to see how he behaved in practices and behind the locker room doors. It's not a pretty sight. Knight screams and yells and throws fits and harasses and verbally abuses his players—and that's when he's in a good mood.

Witness what occurred to Daryl Thomas, a 6'7" center on the 1985–86 Indiana team. Unhappy with how he was playing one day, Knight stopped practice to ridicule him, and Feinstein was there to record what Bobby said:

"Daryl, get the fuck out of my sight. If that's the best you can give us after two day's rest, get away from me. There is absolutely no way you'll start on Saturday. No way. You cost yourself that chance by fucking around. You are so terrible, it's just awful. I don't know what the fuck you are thinking about. You think I was mad last year? You saw me, I was the maddest sonuvabitch you ever saw. You want another year like that? Just get the fuck out of my sight."

After throwing Thomas out of practice, Knight later relented and let him back into a scrimmage. Then he threw him out again: "Daryl, get in the game or get out. Do you know you haven't scored a basket inside since Jesus Christ was lecturing in Omaha? Just get out, Daryl." Turning to his assistants, Knight added dismissively, "Get him the fuck in the locker room. He hasn't done a fucking thing since we got here."

Following practice, the team (including the humiliated Thomas) met to watch a videotape of practice. This set Knight off once more: "Daryl," he told him, "you know you are a fucking joke. I have no more confidence in your ability to go out and play hard than I did when you were a freshman. I don't know how you've fucked up your head in the last two weeks but you're as fucked up now as you've ever been. I wouldn't turn you loose in a game if you were the last guy I had, because of your fucking head. This is just bullshit."

But amazingly, Knight wasn't through yet. He had one more diatribe left. Standing up to stop the tape, he let his junior center have it with all guns blazing: "Daryl, look at that. You don't even run back down the floor hard. That's all I need to know about you, Daryl. All you want to be out there is comfortable. You don't work, you don't sprint back. You know what you are, Daryl? You are the worst fucking pussy I've ever seen play basketball at this school. The absolute worst pussy ever. You have more goddamn ability than 95 percent of the players we've had here but you are a pussy from the top of your head to the bottom of your feet. An absolute fucking pussy. That's my assessment of you after three years."

Bobby Criticizes More of His Players

Barry McDermott once joked that Bobby Knight had all of his players over for Thanksgiving dinner—and he served bread and water. Here are some more instances of Bobby picking on his players—not just poor Daryl Thomas:

Confronting Winston Morgan, a 6'4" senior guard, before a big game: "If that's the kind of crap you're going to give us Wednesday, Winston, don't even bother practicing because you're wasting everyone's time. I just don't want to see any of that garbage like I saw up at Wisconsin. I just hope God takes note of the fact that I coached Winston Morgan for five years."

Ridiculing a player's defense: "Stew, you look like a goddamn dog chasing a rabbit through a briar patch."

To a player who tried to catch a pass with one hand: "Andre, there is no room for one-handed basketball on this team. If God had wanted you to play this game with one hand, you would have an arm growing out of your ass."

At halftime, to two of his rebounders: "This is not fucking junior college. You guys have something go wrong and you sulk and pout. That doesn't go over very big with me. Jadlow, you are just flopping around on the boards like a great white whale. You let them get five rebounds that you had your hands on."

And, questioning the leadership abilities of two other players: "Personally, I don't think the two of you could lead a whore to bed."

Steve Alford

One thing you have to say about Knight: he doesn't play favorites. He trashes all of his players equally, or at least according to how much he thinks they can take. One of the greatest players in Indiana history was Steve Alford. Prep star, Olympic gold medal winner, college All-American, and a senior member of IU's 1987 NCAA championship team, he had one of the purest and best jump shots in the game's history. Nevertheless Coach Knight ragged on him constantly, mainly about his *defense.*

"Steve," Knight told him in practice one day, "you can't stand there like a fucking statue. That's what they've got in the harbor in New York—a fucking statue. I don't need that bullshit in here." At a speech to the Indiana student body at the start of Alford's sophomore year (just months after Steve had played on the Knight-coached 1984 gold medal U.S. Olympic team), Knight told the assembly, "If any of you pass Steve Alford on campus, I want you to stop him and ask him if he can spell *defense.*"

A year later, in 1985, Indiana lost a close, tough game to Kentucky in an early-season showdown of nationally ranked powers. Alford didn't play in the game, having been suspended for one game because of an NCAA rules infraction. Knight was livid about this, and he singled out Alford for his transgression at their next practice. "Alford," he said, "you really cost us that game on Saturday, and I want you to know that I really resent it. I can't forget it. I'm just out of patience with you. What you did was stupid. It wasn't a mistake, it was just plain stupid. You've been told and fucking told and fucking retold, and you screwed up and cost us a game.

"This is a habit with you," Knight continued. "You don't listen, whether it's playing defense or playing hard or this. I don't know if anyone else in here does, but I resent it and it pisses me off. Because of you we lost to a chickenshit operation. I won't forget that."

By Alford's senior year—the championship year—Knight was still chewing on him for his defensive failings, this time, after a loss to Vanderbilt, in a diatribe that also targeted guard Keith Smart. "That has got to be the worst defensive play by two Indiana guards I have ever seen. I can almost excuse Keith, because he's new. But Alford, what's your excuse? How can anybody play four years in this system and not learn one thing about playing defense?" Knight shook his head, concluding, "I've wasted, totally wasted, three years trying to teach you, and the minute you go into a defensive crouch I hear people laughing in the stands."

Bobby Assesses Some of His Past Indiana Basketball Squads

On a senior-dominated team of a few years ago: "Every time we play a fucking game I want to throw up at the way we've recruited for three years."

To a mid-eighties team, while drawing a heart on a chalkboard during halftime: "Does anyone in here know what that is? Huh? I wouldn't think anyone in here would know what that is because it's a heart and no one in here has any. You just played 20 minutes of basketball that was totally devoid of heart. You've played like losers, you've acted like losers, you've wimped, you've whined, you've been sick, you cry, you're hurt. I hope you're proud of yourselves. I really wonder if you care about winning."

Sizing up the coming season with one of his teams: "There is no way you can play basketball like this and beat anybody on our schedule. Not anybody. Not one of the 28 games we play could you win. I couldn't make a schedule easy enough for you to win."

On his 1985 squad, just before it lost to UCLA in the NIT finals: "What I like best about this team right now is the fact that I only have to watch it play one more time."

Bobby Knight Theater

Friends and enemies of Knight have a term to describe the mind games that Knight plays on his charges: "Bobby Knight Theater." The man certainly does have a flair for the dramatic. Fred Taylor, who coached Knight when he played for Ohio State, tells a story about him from the 1979 Pan American Games. That was when Knight was arrested for allegedly assaulting a Puerto Rican policeman during a dispute over practice time. Due to the arrest and the controversy that followed, the U.S. squad was unable to hold a practice before its championship game with Puerto Rico. Nevertheless, with the unrepentant Knight on the sidelines, the Americans beat Puerto Rico to win the title.

After the game, Knight and Taylor (an assistant coach for the games) walked into the Puerto Rican locker room. The governor of Puerto Rico was there. Reporters were there. The beaten Puerto Rican players were there. Suddenly, with the unexpected presence of Knight in the room, the whole place fell quiet.

"I just want to say this," Bobby said. "If we'd had any practice this week, we'd have beaten you by 40."

Thoughts from Bobby

On surviving in the Indiana basketball program: "There are really only two words you need to know to play ball in this program: 'Yes sir.'"

On his temperament: "When patience was handed out, there was a long line, and when I stopped for my dose, I'm not sure I got all of it."

On his favorite word: "I just think *fuck* is the most expressive word in the English language. It can be used to express surprise, as in 'Well, I'll be *fucked*!' Or it can be used to express anger, as in 'Fuck you.' Or it can express dismay, as in 'Oh, *fuck*!'"

On being asked whether blacks were more gifted than whites in basketball: "What a bullshit question. Anyone can play basketball, black, white, blue, or green. You can think of a better question than that."

On coaching in the pros: "Hell, I don't even watch the pros. If the NBA was on Channel 5 and a bunch of frogs making love were on Channel 4, I'd watch the frogs—even if they came in fuzzy."

Speaking to an IU alumni group: "You know, I wish all alumni would be canonized. Then we coaches would only have to kiss your rings."

On the role of religion in basketball: "God couldn't care less if we won or not. He is not going to parachute through the roof of this building and score when we need points."

On basketball in Indiana: "Basketball may have been invented in Massachusetts, but it was made for Indiana."

Indiana—or Nothing

Bobby Knight's disdain for all schools that are not Indiana is legendary. One time he led a mule wearing a Purdue hat onto the set of his television show. The jackass, he explained to the audience, was "someone who is here to represent Purdue's point of view."

Proud of his "clean" program at Indiana, Knight has taken jabs at other schools that have run afoul of the NCAA. He said a few years ago that Indiana's grand rivalry with Kentucky had lost meaning "because of all the crap that's gone down here [in Kentucky] in recruiting over the years." Another scandal-plagued school was Big Ten rival Illinois. At a roast for Bo Schembechler, who was then president of the baseball Detroit Tigers, Knight cracked, "He must be thinking, 'We're paying millions to guys who don't play well.' He must think he's coaching at Illinois."

Some years ago Knight got wind that Indiana prep star Tion McCoy was thinking about choosing Oklahoma or Maryland over IU. This represented heresy to Knight, and in speaking personally to McCoy, he ladled on the sarcasm and ridicule: "Why don't you go play at Oklahoma?" he told the high schooler. "The last time we played them they had Wayman Tisdale and a lot more talent than us, and we beat them by 15. Or Maryland would be great. The last time we played them they had Buck Williams and Albert King and we only beat them by 35. You want to be a good player, Tion? Those are the places for you." Tion apparently agreed. He chose Maryland.

The One That Got Away

The greatest basketball player in Indiana history did not play for the University of Indiana; he played for lowly Indiana State. His name was Larry Bird, of course, and lovers of the game can only speculate what would have happened if the unassuming country boy from French Lick had ever gotten together with the Tyrant of Bloomington. Bird did actually enter Indiana U., in 1974, after being recruited by Knight. "If you're trying to decide between Indiana State and IU," Knight told him with his typical disdain for other schools, "then you don't belong at IU." Well, the skittish Birdman came, but flew the roost after only 24 days at the school. IU was too large, too unfriendly, not his style at all. "Thirty-three thousand people is not my idea of a school, it's a country," Bird said, explaining why he was leaving.

Knight has said that if he had known what type of player Larry would turn out to be, he'd have made more of an effort to make him stay. Bird himself has expressed admiration for Knight, saying that if he had stayed he might have become an even better player. But one observer close to the scene thinks differently. She thinks that if Larry had stayed and tried to fit into Knight's unyielding system, it would have destroyed him as an original basketball talent. "Larry's a leader, and Bobby Knight would've changed him," says Georgia Bird, Larry's mother. She adds, "Bobby Knight doesn't recruit the boys for what they can do. He molds them into what he wants. I don't think that would have ever worked with Larry. I think he would have ruined Larry."

Dale Brown Hates Bobby Knight . . .

Dale Brown, the basketball coach for Louisiana State University, has called Bobby Knight "a truly evil, cunning, and sick person." One of their epic confrontations occurred in 1987, when LSU lost by one point to Indiana in the NCAA tournament after leading by a wide margin early in the game. Brown blamed the defeat in large part on Knight, who put on one of his classic temper tantrums and drew a technical but also, in Brown's view, intimidated the referees so much that it cost LSU the game.

Years later, Brown was still seething about it. "He should have been out of the game, gone," he told John Feinstein. "He stole that game from us. He intimidated the officials. Everyone in the country knows it, but no one will say it. Well, I'll say it. I want that son of a bitch to know there's one guy who isn't afraid of him. I want to play him anywhere, anytime, but he won't do it. And before the game I'd like the two of us to be locked in a wrestling room naked by ourselves and let's see which one of us comes out."

. . . And Vice Versa

"Had he been drinking?"

> —*Bobby Knight*, referring to Brown, after Brown predicted that the winner of the LSU–Indiana game in the 1992 NCAA tournament would become the national champion

"I was worried about losing until I looked down the floor and saw Dale Brown. Then I knew we had a chance."
—*Bobby Knight*, about that stormy 1987 game with LSU

Two Instances in Which Knight Is Compared to Famous Figures in World War II

Bobby is just a basketball coach, but he and his fans like to think of him in grander, more historic terms. Here's a sample from one of Knight's fans, writing to the *Indianapolis Star*: "Like General Patton in World War II, Knight knows how to shape boys into men and naturally this bothers all the people who would like men to be wimps and sissies. They would prefer someone like Alan Alda, who is sensitive, caring, supporting and vulnerable. Sorry, wimps."

Of course, there are some people—wimps, probably—who, when they think of Knight, tend to compare him to a somewhat different World War II personage. Explaining why a young southern California prep star, Richard Mandeville of La Canada High, decided to attend Indiana, Mark Whicker writes, "Mandeville took one trip to Bloomington and was spellbound. Similarly, Bobby Knight visited La Canada and got all misty, like he did the first time he read *Mein Kampf*."

Bobby Knight on Sportswriters

"All of us learn to write by the second grade. Then most of us go on to other things."

"I can't think of a more dishonest business in this country than newspapers."

More of Bobby's Thoughts

While addressing an alumni group, on Big Ten Commissioner Wayne Duke: "You know, if any of you someday are on the street and you see that Wayne Duke is about to get run over by a car, I would encourage you, I think, to save him. But not if it's in any way inconvenient for you to do so."

To referee Tom Rucker, after an Indiana victory: "Hey Rucker, have you figured out the difference between a block and a charge yet? You think I'm kidding, don't you? Why don't you do everybody a favor and just quit? You make everyone in the game look bad. It's not funny, Rucker, the only funny thing about it is that you're a goddamn joke."

On trash-talking by basketball players: "That kind of ———— from the players reflects on the entire operation of a team. I'd rather have players concentrating on what we're going to do than on some clever, wiseass thing to say to somebody else."

After one of his favorite players, Quinn Buckner, was cut by the Indiana Pacers: "Buckner contributes so much to any team that understands basketball. He gets everybody to play better. It's a damn shame in a state like this that loves good basketball that we have a professional organization up in Indianapolis that clearly doesn't understand anything about the game."

On future pro star Wayman Tisdale, whom Knight coached on the 1984 U.S. Olympic team: "He does one or two things acceptable by my standards."

Another future pro, Charles Barkley, was cut by Knight from that 1984 Olympic team. Before the trials Knight was asked if he'd ask the beefy Auburn star to lose weight. Said Knight: "Asking Charles Barkley to get down to 215 pounds would be like asking Raquel Welch to undergo plastic surgery."

Upon resigning as president of the National Association of Basketball Coaches: "I'm through sitting next to people who talk sanctimoniously about our business, then go out and break the rules. Earlier this year (1986), I got a letter from an administrator at Illinois, complaining about my referring to their athletic program as a 'mess.' In my reply, I pointed out that in the 12 years I've been at Indiana, they've been on probation four times and have been investigated on three other occasions. 'If there's a better word in the English language than *mess* to describe that situation,' I wrote, 'please advise me as to what it is and I'll use it. Instead of scolding me, why don't you apologize to the rest of us for cheating?' I'm still waiting to hear back from him."

On women and violence: "If rape is inevitable, relax and enjoy it." (This remark of Knight's, made to Connie Chung on national

TV, stirred up a considerable controversy. Knight later apologized.)
Knight's son Pat, an Indiana University player, was dismissed from the team after being arrested for public drunkenness. After Pat was reinstated, his father said: "Pat Knight is a living example of why some animals eat their young."

Final Words on Bobby

"Bobby Knight doesn't have ulcers, but he's a carrier."
—*Johnny Kerr*, ex–NBA coach

"Bobby Knight is a good friend of mine. But if I ever need a heart transplant, I want his. It's never been used."
—*George Raveling*, USC basketball coach

Coaches

Coaches are coaches. The college coaches do more teaching and have to recruit, while the pro guys have to know how to handle massive egos inflated by massive salaries. But essentially, coaching is coaching—whether it is in the NBA, NCAA, CBA, or CYO. In this chapter we take a look at both pro and college coaches, and some of the headaches they must endure while watching the game from the bench.

Rupp Stuff

One of the orneriest fellows ever to coach a college basketball game was Adolph Rupp, who, coincidentally enough, also happens to be the winningest coach in college basketball history. Rupp coached at the University of Kentucky for over 40 years. Much like Bobby Knight, he was feared by his players for his hard-guy disciplinary techniques, his angry outbursts, his outright cruelty. But, like Knight, his wicked sarcasm was often laced with a biting sort of humor. Some samples from the legendary Rupp canon:

After one of his Wildcat players got a rebound during practice: "Rose! You look like a Shetland pony in a stud horse parade. Stop practice, everyone, take a shower. We're going to have a successful season now. Rose got a rebound!"

After a Kentucky player, who had missed practice due to the death of his grandmother, returned to the team: "My God, boys, we're not going to continue playing like this. This is war! And another thing. We're not going to have any more of this grandmother dying business."

Addressing a player at halftime in a game in which Kentucky was trailing: "Ed, I want you to go to the hotel right now and write me a letter, no, write me a theme, no, better make that a doctoral dissertation on this subject: 'Why Adolph Rupp was crazy enough to go to the state of Georgia after the likes of you.' "

After one of his stars played poorly in a close Kentucky win in Philadelphia, Rupp told him, "Mobley, would you please go back to the middle of the floor and just sit there until I can get the hell out of this place?" When the player said he didn't understand the instructions, Rupp clarified, "I want you to be able to tell the folks back in Lexington that you did something good and constructive here in Philadelphia."

Pat Riley, then a star at Kentucky, was knocked to the floor while trying for a rebound, and slid almost directly under his coach on the sidelines. Rupp looked down on him and glowered, "Pat, get your ass up! There goes your man with the ball!"

Coaches Talk About Other Coaches

It may be a surprise to some, but not all members of the college coaching fraternity love or respect one another. As proof, we offer the following:

"He's a phony, lying, plastic chickenshit asshole. His holier-than-thou attitude about Notre Dame and how it's superior to other schools bothers me. I'm an Irish Catholic, so don't tell me I'm against Irish Catholics. But he acts like we know more than you do, and we're more important than you. They aren't any more important than Sonoma State. They're going to heaven, and you and me aren't? I think that's the way he purports himself. He's a dog as far as I'm concerned."
—former San Francisco–area basketball coach *Brad Duggan*, on Notre Dame's Digger Phelps

"We'll play anyone but Pitt. I'd like to play them but [Pitt coach] Paul Evans has said some negative things about our players and so I won't play Pitt as long as he's the coach."
—*Digger Phelps*

"That's just typical Digger. He doesn't want to play us so he makes an excuse like that. Then he'll schedule Robert Morris when he comes to Pittsburgh rather than play us. Look at his schedule now.

He plays half the ECC [East Coast Conference] and half the Ivy
League."
> —*Paul Evans*, responding to Phelps's criticism

"They let John Thompson run everything at the school. He's more
powerful than the athletic director and the president. The athletic
director says he wants to play Maryland and Thompson says no,
they don't play. It's unbelievable."
> —*Paul Evans*, angry after a fight broke out between his
> Pitt squad and Georgetown during a Big East game

"I think what he did was unethical. I just think it's wrong."
> —Tennessee coach *Don DeVoe*, on LSU's Dale Brown
> hiring Stanley Roberts's high school coach to get Stan-
> ley to come to LSU (asked to respond, Brown said, "I
> think divorce is unethical," in a jab at DeVoe's divorce
> and remarriage)

"Denny Crum stated that the high school coach picked up the
tab for dinner. I was really happy to hear about that. High school
coaches, because of their exorbitant salaries, always pick up the
tab for college coaches."
> —Kentucky's coach *Rick Pitino*, about a dinner meet-
> ing between Louisville's Crum and prep star Dwayne
> Morton and his high school coach (Morton, to Pitino's
> dismay, signed with Louisville, though the meeting
> was in violation of NCAA rules)

After Jim Valvano was named athletic director at North Carolina
State in addition to his duties as basketball coach, Denny Crum
criticized the move, saying that he didn't think anyone could handle both jobs. Said Valvano in reply: "That's why we didn't interview Denny."

"It would've been much better for Jim Valvano and for college
basketball if he had lost that national championship in 1983. Because Valvano's biggest moment, in my opinion, turned out to be

the beginning of his downfall. Let me ask you a question: Do you really think he had any other priority than winning basketball games? No. End of discussion. Now he sends in his agent. Education isn't done through an agent. It's you and me, coach and school. As soon as a coach sends an agent in, he removes himself from being an educator."

> —*Bobby Knight*, on Jim Valvano, who resigned at North Carolina State amid scandal and allegations of cheating

Other College Coaches We Have Known

"Rick told me he had lost 35 pounds. For Rick, that's like losing an earlobe."

> —*Al McGuire*, on Utah coach Rick Majerus (who once was so hefty, he said, that he ordered his clothes from a "tent and awning supply house")

"Insiders claim that Arizona coach Lute Olson has made no friends in the Pac-10. Knowing Olson, that's not really a surprise."

> —*Terry Boers*, Chicago columnist

"Louie Carnesecca speaks fluent Italian, and Rollie Massimino thinks he does. One night, in a restaurant, Rollie decides to order dinner for us. The waiter came back with three umbrellas."

> —*Jim Valvano*, on two of his former coaching colleagues

"It's a tossup as to what is uglier: Lou Carnesecca's sweaters or the Redmen's record."

> —*Gene Wojciechowski*, on St. John's 1992 season

"Dean Smith is the only person able to hold Michael Jordan to less than 20 points a game."

> —joke about North Carolina's Dean Smith and his control style of offense, back in the days when the great Jordan was playing for him

"I'm a no-nonsense coach who took over a nonsense program."
—*Don DeVoe*, explaining why he was quitting as Florida
basketball coach in 1990

"You know, if a hemorrhoid could talk, it would sound just like
Jim Boeheim."
—a reporter, on the whiny voice of the Syracuse coach

Howard Speaks!

Howard Cosell has had his opinions about college basketball,
just as he has had his opinions about everything else. He has accused college basketball of sacrificing education and of corrupting young men at the altar of big-time, big-money athletics.
He has blamed hypocritical university administrators as well as
the NCAA for this, but he also thinks that many college basketball coaches are to blame, too. In his book *What's Wrong with
Sports*, he blasted some of the biggest names in the coaching fraternity.

On former Maryland coach Lefty Driesell: "This snake oil selling, slick-talking huckster is a disgrace to the sport and to education as a whole."

On Temple coach John Chaney: "A national disgrace. . . . This
man Chaney is a dangerous thinker. He receives absolution from
Temple alum Bill Cosby, a man who would better serve blacks by
taking a stronger stand on education."

On Larry Brown: "Perhaps the most notorious job jumping
coach."

On Clemson's Tates Locke, who was involved in recruitment scan-
dals in the 1970s: "This pill popping, hard-drinking, coed-chasing
former head coach."

On Jim Valvano, former NC State coach: "Valvano, a flashy, show
business type, attracts trouble, much of his own making."

And, on Valvano's most notorious recruit: "Valvano had be-
smirched himself by the recruitment and support of Chris Washburn, a druggie and a petty thief, and a discredit to society as a
whole. Washburn belonged in a correctional facility or a rehabili-
tation center, not in an institution of higher learning."

The Evils of Recruiting:
A Few Thoughts from the Coaches

The worst thing about being a college basketball coach is having to recruit. You need to be a con artist—willing to say anything and promise just as much—to be a successful recruiter. Recruiting is degrading, corrupting, and cutthroat. But don't take our word for it. Just listen to college coaches themselves.

"It's demeaning. I have to go in and sell myself and my university. Why should I have to do that to a 17-year-old kid? Why should I answer his questions, many of which are totally ridiculous."
—*Jim Valvano* (North Carolina State)

"In the middle of our talk, the kid said to me, 'Coach, how many seats are there in your new arena and how many times will you be on television next year?' I just snapped. I said to him, 'Look, you can't even read and write and you're asking me how many times you're going to be on television? You've got some nerve.' "
—*Ed Tapscott* (American University)

"What we really are, all of us, is a bunch of white slavers going to Africa to bring back the biggest, best studs we can find."
—*Dale Brown* (LSU)

"A lot of coaches will lie to you and say their graduation rates are highest. But coaches will tell you anything. You can't believe them."
—*Jerry Tarkanian* (UNLV)

"You know, Chris, I'm sitting here telling you what a good guy I am, and why you should come play for me, and how I care about people, and how I care about my players. If I was everything I'm telling you I am, I'd be working for Mother Teresa. I wouldn't be sitting here recruiting you. And let's face it. Recruiting is nothing but hypocrisy."
—*Dale Brown*

"If you are a decent human being on any level you must hate what we do in recruiting."
—*Jim Valvano*

Cheating? Who Cheats?

Still, even though NCAA recruiting is rife with corruption and deceit, people still play by the rules. Fair is fair, and no major college coach or administrator would dare think about bending the rules in order to sign that McDonald's All-America blue-chip prospect who is going to turn the program around and make tens of thousands of dollars, if not hundreds of thousands of dollars, for the university. Right? Uh, right?

"It's just like speeding. Everyone does it at one time or another. Just a few get caught."
—*JohnWhisenant*, assistant coach, University of New Mexico

"The bottom line is that everyone cheats. The question is, to what extent? And if the Cats are going to compete on a big-time level for the best recruits, they're going to have to play the game."
—*Alan Cutler*, Lexington, Kentucky, broadcaster

"The point of the commentary was to let people know cheating was still going on all over the country. I'm not suggesting that Kentucky goes out and cheats. What I'm saying is, there are players who won't come here because Kentucky won't cheat. There's a big difference between the two."
—*Alan Cutler*, backpedaling rapidly after a controversy erupted over his remarks about cheating. (Shortly thereafter, Cutler's TV station cut back on his airtime. "By reducing Cutler's chances to put his foot in his mouth," *Sports Illustrated* commented, "the station probably did him a favor.")

"What's the big deal? Let Driesell get the kid a bigger car. Hell, I'll get him a fucking Sherman tank if he wants one."
—University of New Mexico coach *Norm Ellenberger,* on hearing reports that Driesell and Maryland had successfully wooed high school star Moses Malone with promises of a new Chrysler (Malone eventually jumped straight to the pros)

Thoughts on the NCAA

"As crooked an organization as there is in this country."
—*Dale Brown*, LSU basketball coach

"The NCAA will get so mad at Kentucky that it will slap Cleveland State with two more years of probation."
—UNLV coach *Jerry Tarkanian,* at the time of Kentucky's recruiting scandal under coach Eddie Sutton

"They are an organization out of control. If they don't like you, they can bury you."
—*Terry Giles*, attorney for Jerry Tarkanian in his lawsuit against the NCAA

"Even if I wasn't an athlete, I'd be appalled. From [NCAA executive director Dick] Schultz on down, they're a group of unaware people trying to follow the 1930s status quo. First, they don't acknowledge that college teams are really professional franchises. The universities recruit the players and push them through the system so fast that they have no chance to get their degree."
—*Elmore Spencer*, former center for UNLV

"And those damn bureaucrats mouth off about standards, but I don't see the billion dollars from the television contract go to the small schools to help them fight deficits. I see a new NCAA office complex go up in Kansas City with new everything, all the way down to the company stationery. They probably fly first class now instead of economy when they go to investigate schools. And a

coach can't give a player dinner even if he might need it for nutritional reasons? I think I could swallow the vomit better if they weren't so hypocritical."
>—more from *Elmore Spencer*

"I hate to say this, because I'm an athletic director, but there are not many rocket scientists in our group making these decisions."
>—DePaul athletic director *Bill Bradshaw*, speaking about an NCAA committee investigating alleged recruiting violations by UNLV

A Few Intemperate Remarks by Coaches About the Men with the Whistles and Striped Shirts

"Did the guy think that 14,000 people came to the damn game to see him work? Did he think all eyes were on him? What crap that is. . . . That's the problem with so many of these goddamn guys. They think they're the fucking stars."
>—*Jim Valvano*, then with North Carolina State

"They just choked. They're cheaters. The police escorting them off the court should have escorted them to jail."
>—Louisiana Tech coach *Jerry Lloyd*, blaming the refs for a one-point loss

"I've been around the game a long time, and what you saw tonight is a crime. The way the officiating is in college basketball is unbelievable. I guarantee when they play an ACC school, like a Duke or a North Carolina, they won't shoot 44 free throws. The way it is takes all the fun out of it for the kids."
>—Howard coach *Butch Beard*, after his club shot 16 free throws to Maryland's 44 in a 1993 loss to the Terrapins

"The officiating in our league is awful, but that was the worst out there. The officiating in our league is a terrible problem that has to be addressed."
>—*Tates Locke*, Indiana State coach, after throwing his money clip and wallet onto the court to protest a call

"I did find out one thing: why it took so many Mexicans to win, to beat our guys at the Alamo. I just found that out today, because one of them was working the game."
—*Tates Locke*, after the same game, speaking about referee Willie Sanchez (both Locke and the university apologized afterward for his statements)

After Oklahoma coach Billy Tubbs was assessed for a T in the 1989 Big Eight championship game with Missouri, the irate fans in Norman pelted the gymnasium floor with trash and other objects. Asked by the refs to say something to try to quiet the crowd, Tubbs took a microphone and announced, "The referees have asked that, regardless of how terrible the officiating is, please don't throw things on the floor." This brought a new shower of debris from the fans, and made the refs livid. For this, Tubbs was named "Bush League Coach of the Century" by *Referee* magazine.

Have Whistle, Will Travel: Some Thoughts on the Man Who Has Coached at UCLA, Kansas, New Jersey, San Antonio, Los Angeles, Etc.

Larry Brown is the perfect segue from college coaching to the pros. He's coached in both places; matter of fact, is there any place he hasn't coached?

"I wanted to be like Larry Brown when I was growing up. I walked like him. I talked like him. I even moved four times."
—*Billy Crystal*

"Larry Brown should be ready to leave the Clippers anytime now. He's already been with them four seasons—winter, spring, summer, and fall."
—Joke

"Larry was always playing mind games with us. He was the kind of guy who made sure he hit you in the soft spots. Before games he would pump us up about how we were going to kill the opposing player, and when we didn't he would come to us after the game

and tell us how the guy kicked our ass. I know a lot of us weren't sad to see Brown move on."
—*Darryl Dawkins*, who played for Brown at New Jersey

"Larry believes everything he says when he's saying it. It's just that five minutes later, he may believe something completely different."
—a friend of Brown's, as quoted by author John Feinstein

"Larry is a very good basketball coach. I don't think any of us need to debate that. But he has to at least admit he has done some things wrong. Larry sits on television and says, 'I've never done anything wrong.' He's two for two in getting programs placed on probation. And I think if Larry were to sit down with you, he'd say, 'I care about my players. I care about my program. I care about college basketball.' At that moment he would; five minutes later, though, he would care about something else."
—*John Feinstein*

Dick Motta Talks About Coaching in the NBA

"I lie awake some nights trying to decide whether this team [the Dallas Mavericks] is a grown child who's ready to go to college and doesn't need me anymore or whether this is still a baby that needs to be nurtured and fed."

"Right now, Ralph [Sampson] is not helping us. He just clogs things up. If he's crippled and can't help us, I've got to know by the end of the year. I'm going to keep playing him. I'm just going to plod along with him." (Sampson was eventually released from another of Motta's teams, the Sacramento Kings.)

"It's all over the league. My son Kip works for Seattle, and he says he has three players coming up to him every day griping about [coach] K. C. Jones and playing time. If it keeps going like this, authority is going to mean nothing in this league."

"I know I have more knowledge of basketball in my little finger than any of the players have in their whole bodies."

After being fired by the Kings: "I felt like a drowning man willing to grab anything they threw to me. It turned out they threw me razor blades."

. . . While Others Talk About Motta

"I don't know why we practice. We ain't ever going to win a game. Coach just sits there on the sidelines, never talks. Just blows his whistle."
> —*Spud Webb*, guard for the Sacramento Kings when Motta coached there

"Dick Motta continues to complain in Sacramento that despite five number-one draft choices in the last two years and trades for Mitch Richmond and Spud Webb, the Kings still are hampered by a lack of talent. But then, Motta was the guy who once wanted to trade Rolando Blackman for Lewis Lloyd, so talent evaluation is not his strength."
> —*Jan Hubbard*, columnist

"Motta's conservative (boring) half court offense isn't working. The players are better suited for a quicker game, but the stubborn old buzzard won't back down. . . . See Dick plod. See Sacramento lose."
> —*Steve Tady*, sportswriter

"Motta had a peculiar way of treating players. . . . Keep them in the dark. Keep your thumb on them. Intimidate them when possible."
> —*Jan Hubbard*

"Guys were frustrated with Dick's head games. He would talk to players and then go talk to other players and say they had said things about each other."
> —*Spud Webb*, Kings guard

"I don't think there is any doubt that the players didn't give their full effort. I think they went out to get him, and they got him. That may not be right, but that's what it had come to."
                    —*Rick Benner*, Kings president, after Motta was fired
                        during the 1992 season

"It was a gut check. We talked about roles. We talked about what each of us could do to help the team. I told the guys, 'You don't know how lucky you are to be playing for a guy like Saint. We had Dick Motta here, and you know what that was like."
                    —*Spud Webb*, discussing a 1993 Kings team meeting
                        after Gary St. Jean was hired as coach to replace Motta

Wes Unseld

Before becoming an NBA coach, Wes Unseld was a 6'7" over-achieving forward who starred for the Washington Bullets in the 1970s. He's seen some changes in the game over the years. For one, there is far more kissing than there used to be. "Can you imagine guys kissing on the court?" he said, referring to the famous pecks between Isiah Thomas and Magic Johnson in their championship games against each other. "Can you imagine me kissing Willis Reed? I don't think they'd let Willis back in Louisiana. They wouldn't let me back in my neighborhood."

Unlike some of the old-timers who just carp about the game to-day while sentimentalizing about the days of yore, Unseld has brought his considerable presence back to the game as a coach. Though often pitted against taller competitors, Wes was never afraid to throw his weight around when he was a player. The same is true now that he's coaching. A couple of years ago he nearly came to blows with Indiana Pacers coach Dick Versace. "Credit the security people in Landover, Maryland, with a real save for getting be-tween coaches Wes Unseld of Washington and Dick Versace of Indiana," says Terry Boers, who was an eyewitness to the episode. "If Unseld had gotten his hands on the Pacer boss, Versace no longer would have just looked like a Q-tip—he would have been one."

Wes is also not shy about criticizing what he sees as overly phys-

"Oh, fellas! Say, fellas!" Wes Unseld is an old-school coach who does not believe in kissing among NBA players. (Photo by Mitchell Layton)

ical play. After watching Charles Barkley do his thing against the Bullets, Unseld fumed, "He just ducks his head and bowls people over. He barrels right over them, and nothing is called." But Barkley, who grew up watching Unseld play, had the best possible reply: "Wes should know. He's my role model. Everything I do under the basket I learned from him."

Other Pro Coaches We Have Known

"If there is an addition by subtraction, the Wolves did it by firing Bill Musselman, whose slow-down, mind-numbing, trash-talking tactics made NBA basketball a veritable unpleasant experience."
—*George Shirk*, sportswriter

"It was the right choice. He couldn't find home plate with a geiger counter."
> —*Bill Fitch*, on Bulls coach Phil Jackson, who, as a youngster, once debated whether to pursue a basketball career or become a baseball pitcher

"If you can't work for K. C. Jones in this league, you can't play. You should go home every night and thank your lucky stars. All that he asks of anybody is to show up and play. . . . It's a dark day in the NBA when a guy like K. C. is no longer working. This is not a baby-sitting service. We're grown men. If you come into this league and need a kick in the butt every night, you don't belong in it. K. C. treated you like a man, like an adult."
> —*Kevin McHale*, after his former coach was fired by Seattle in 1992

"When the Sonics hired K. C. Jones, he had the reputation as a coach who was not a strong disciplinarian. Last week, the Sonics fired Jones, in part, because he wasn't a strong disciplinarian. They also fired him despite owing him $500,000 a year for the next three and a half seasons. It doesn't appear that they used a lot of discipline during their contract negotiations, either."
—*Jan Hubbard*, columnist

"To paraphrase Westhead's favorite playwright: All the world's a stage, and he's going to soon wish he was on one."
—columnist *Terry Boers*, assessing Paul Westhead's prospects taking over as coach of the Denver Nuggets (Westhead has since been canned)

"George Karl's hairline has receded so much that he shows the tape of each game to the Sonics on his forehead."
—*Peter Vecsey*, on the Sonics coach

"That's Pat. He's got the arrogance and confidence. That's the way he looks at himself—as a star."
—*Magic Johnson*, on his former coach Pat Riley

When he came to coach in New York, Pat Riley did not heed Rick Bonnell's advice to lose his famous "wet look" hairstyle. Explains Bonnell: "In L.A. slick hair means culture. In New York it means your late uncle is buried under Giants Stadium." (Photo by Joe Gosen)

"They'll run longer than the Energizer bunny, burn out score-boards, excel on their home court, get to the playoffs, then fizzle out."

> —sportswriter *Paul Ladewski*, speculating on what the 76ers would be like under head coach Doug Moe

"It has been proven historically in the business world that people tend to perform better when they look their best and act their best. Not only in the business world, but in the sports world. Look at Doug Moe. He and Frank Layden. They have consistently been the worst dressed and how many championships have they won?"

> —*George Shinn*, Charlotte owner

Fashion Victims: NBA Coaches

In the NBA, there are men like Chuck Daly and Pat Riley, and then there are men like Doug Moe and Don Nelson. "I watch the way Nellie dresses," says Mike Dunleavy, coach of the Milwaukee Bucks and a friend of Nelson's, "and I try to stay as far away from that as possible." Doug Moe is another NBA coach with about as much fashion flair as a bag lady. After being named coach of the Denver Nuggets, Dan Issel said that his two role models in coaching were the late Adolph Rupp of Kentucky and Doug Moe. "In honor of Coach Rupp, I will wear a brown suit at my first game," he said. "And in honor of Doug, I will wear black shoes with it." Moe's anti–*GQ* style has served as inspiration for other coaches around the league as well. "When things aren't looking good," says Larry Brown, "you can always look at Doug and make yourself feel good."

Intimidating the Refs: One Technique

Does Sarunas Marciulionis of the Golden State Warriors get a bad break from the refs because he's not an American? Don Nelson thought so, and raised a stink about it during the 1991–92 season. "They say he initiates the contact with his style of play," Nelson said in remarks that drew a $3,000 fine from the NBA. "But I say Sarunas hurts just like everybody else, and I'm concerned for his safety." Nelson alleged that Sarunas wasn't getting the calls because he's Lithuanian and played for the Soviet Union basketball team that defeated the United States and won the gold in the 1988 Olympics.

Two incidents appeared to back up Nelson. In a game in Dallas, reporters at courtside overheard referee Ed Middleton say to Sarunas, after calling him for a double dribble, "Maybe you can put two hands on the ball in Russia, but not here." Another time, Nelson claims to have heard an NBA referee say, "I wouldn't give that Russian a call."

Most NBA observers don't think Sarunas is a victim of nationalism; rather, they think it's a classic case of a coach looking out for one of his players and trying to make the referees give him the benefit of the doubt more often. All coaches—pro, college, wherever—do it all the time, in fact. "Marciulionis gets every break," said one Western Conference general manager. "He walks every time he gets the ball, for one thing. And he does one trick where he puts the ball right in the defender's chest, pushes off and shoots his shot. I think the complaints were all just a ploy by Nellie to get his player more breaks."

One Guy Who Doesn't Think Don Nelson Is a Genius

Conventional wisdom holds that Don Nelson, the Gene Mauch of basketball, is a brilliant basketball thinker and strategist who, but for lack of a big man, would have won any number of NBA titles by now. R. E. Graswich, a writer for the McClatchy newspaper chain, does not subscribe to conventional wisdom. "In 15 years of coaching," he writes, "Nelson made many people believe he's a bona fide basketball genius. We're still awaiting conclusive evidence. His true talent, we've long suspected, is his embrace of public relations."

Graswich asserts that, despite rosters full of talent in Milwaukee and Golden State—Sidney Moncrief, Bob Lanier, Chris Mullin, Tim Hardaway, etc.—Nelson's record in the playoffs is little better than .500. "In 15 years, Nelson coached his way to one fewer title than Dick Motta. Which is to say, Nelson hasn't coached a championship." Graswich continues: "In 1988, Nelson went west and joined the Warriors. He gained credibility by upsetting the Utah

"The Genius," Don Nelson, has received lots of trophies and awards for his coaching. None of them, however, is an NBA championship trophy. (Photo by Brad Mangin)

Jazz in 1989 and stopping the San Antonio Spurs [in 1991]. In both cases, Golden State celebrated its stunning triumphs by folding in the next round.

"All this from a coaching genius. We'd hate to think how Nelson's teams would fare if the coach were merely bright-to-normal," Graswich adds.

Graswich discounts the theory that Nelson intentionally prevents his teams from getting too good, thus raising expectations that he cannot meet. No, Graswich believes that Nelson sincerely wants an NBA title; he simply can't deliver the goods. The writer concludes, "Nelson lacks the patience, personality and luck to guide a championship team. . . . When the NBA finals are contested in June, the teams will feature balance, size, strength, quickness, depth and abundant talent. They will also feature coaches who put on their pants one leg at a time. So much for the Warriors."

Bill Fitch and the New Jersey Mess

Bill Fitch and the New Jersey Nets are a case study in all the things that can go wrong between a coach and his team. Early in the 1991–92 season, after two full seasons under Fitch's leadership, the Nets were an utter and complete mess. "The Nets . . . are not the worst team in the NBA, not while there's a Minnesota Timberwolf still standing for the national anthem anyway. But they remain the most adept at embarrassing themselves," wrote Jack McCallum. "With an ideal franchise, owners, front-office executives, coaches and players are on the same page; in New Jersey, these people are reading different books in different languages."

Known as a controlled offense coach with a lively wit—"We've got a long way to go just to get us to last year, and last year was good enough to get us into the lottery," he remarked during exhibition season—Fitch owns a championship ring from Boston. He is also credited with turning the expansion Cleveland Cavaliers and a sick Houston club into contenders. But his attempt to do the same in New Jersey disintegrated into a bitter feud with his players. "Get off my back!" Dennis Hopson once shouted at him. "If you don't like the way I play, get me out of here." The normally stormy Fitch replied calmly, "Dennis, I'll do my best to accommodate you." "Talk about your civil wars," said Mark Heisler, "this is like Bobby Knight coaching 2 Live Crew." Fitch himself put it another way. Referring to the constant criticism he received from his own players, he observed that "coaching has become a situation where you've got a lot more people who think they know your business. I don't think there's any college with seven presidents."

A good deal of the strife was caused by the selection of Kenny Anderson as the Nets' first pick in the 1991 draft, a choice that Fitch heatedly opposed. The traditionalist coach saw the freewheeling Anderson as an overrated project who would take years before he made an impact in the NBA, if ever. "I'm still waiting to see the player everyone is raving about," Fitch said about Anderson early in the season. He added that drafting Anderson had been "a horrible decision"—a direct shot at Nets co-owner Joe Taub, who had made the choice. Taub and his ownership partners in turn began looking for a replacement for Fitch, and at one point reportedly offered the job to Jim Valvano, the former North Carolina State coach. Fitch, scoffing at Valvano's lack of NBA experience, said, "I'll tell you what. I'd *love* to coach a game seven against Valvano." Valvano did not take the job, though, leaving Fitch to play Captain Bligh as his players mutinied underneath him. The level of scorn the Nets players felt for Fitch was really quite astonishing, even by NBA standards. Here is, for example, Sam Bowie: "If you enjoy following your leader, then the sky's the limit [as a team]. But with this team, and this leader . . . I don't know what direction we're going to go in on any given night. I mean, I've been truly amazed at what we were able to accomplish under these circumstances. But at the same time, we probably should have won 50 games, because we've got such great personnel. Look around— there's nothing but lottery picks here. But we just haven't been a tight unit, because we refuse to play follow the leader. I can't think of a single player here who likes playing for this guy."

The wondrously talented Derrick Coleman had lots of problems with Fitch. After Fitch refused to play him in the first half of a loss to the Los Angeles Lakers, Coleman asked the press, "You call that coaching?" He was even more to the point during a game against Miami. Although he played most of the game, Coleman wouldn't go back in in the final minutes because a groin injury was acting up. When Fitch confronted him, Coleman shot back, "Get out of my face, you pigheaded ———!"

Mookie Blaylock also criticized Fitch, this time for trying to put Chris Morris into a lost cause with only 25 seconds to play. "I can't see putting a starter in with a half minute left. Why do that, after you just pulled him? Does that make any sense?" Blaylock's reputation as a point guard grew under Fitch, but Mookie didn't give his coach any credit for it. "I don't think he should get any credit for doing that," he said. "I give myself the credit. He isn't out there in my shoes."

You wouldn't believe it to listen to them, but the Nets actually made the playoffs in 1992. Still, it wasn't enough to save Fitch, who was dumped at the end of the season in favor of former Piston miracle worker Chuck Daly. Now it's Daly's turn to try to rescue a franchise that, in Frank Deford's words, "has been lost so long not even Ross Perot knows it was ever missing."

Bill Fitch in Cleveland

It hasn't always been so bad for Bill Fitch. Before coming to New Jersey he coached, among other places, in Cleveland. He presided over the expansion Cavaliers in the very first year of their existence, 1970–71, when they won an awesome 15 games. But in Cleveland, as opposed to New Jersey, there were no stars, no grumbling high-priced malcontents. The Cavs weren't expected to win anything. There was far less pressure, and consequently Fitch could exercise, and people could appreciate, his considerable wit.

Asked how he was feeling as the Cavs were losing the first 15 games of the season, Fitch said, "I feel like a guy who has lockjaw and seasickness at the same time." After yet another loss, he added, "Sometimes you wake up in the morning and wish your parents had never met."

When the Cavaliers ventured out West to play a night game against the San Francisco Warriors, Fitch showed up at the back door of the Cow Palace without the proper identification. The security guard didn't recognize him. "Listen, I'm the Cleveland coach," he pleaded. "Who else would be sneaking through the back alleys alone at night?" The security guard, apparently seeing the logic of that, let him in.

After their opening run of 15 losses, Fitch's troops finally won one—against a hapless Portland squad. Fitch's summary of the game: "It looked like gamblers got to both teams." Cleveland went on to win 14 more games that season, and, speaking for the coaches of losing teams everywhere, Fitch said that the Cavs hardly needed his services at all. "What this team needs," he explained, "is a chaplain, not a coach."

Jammin' and Slammin': A Potpourri of NBA Stuff

The rap against the NBA is that, after you strip away Magic and Bird and Michael Jordan and Charles Barkley and maybe the Bad Boys, there aren't any real colorful personalities. That's not the case at all. Although we start with Magic in this chapter, most of our attention is on the Danny Ainges, the James Donaldsons, and the Karl Malones—characters in their own right who are often (and often deservedly) the target of insults.

Magic and Martina

You have to search long and hard for insults about Magic Johnson, but Martina Navratilova kicked up a considerable stir about him after Magic's dramatic announcement in late 1991 that he had the AIDS virus. Most of the reaction concerning Magic was, understandably, of shock and dismay: not only was he being forced out of the game too early, but his life was at risk too.

While expressing sympathy for the great Lakers star, Martina saw "a very big-time double standard" in the reaction both of the public and of the corporations that vowed to retain Magic as their company pitchman. "Like if I had the AIDS virus, would people be understanding?" Martina asked the New York *Post* during a tennis tournament at Madison Square Garden. "No, because they'd say I'm gay. . . . That's why they're accepting it with him because supposedly he got it through heterosexual contact. There have been other athletes who died from AIDS, and they were pushed aside because they either got it from drugs or they were gay." She said that as a gay person, if she had contracted the disease, the public's attitude would be: "She had it coming."

Besides the gay issue, Martina charged that unfair sexual atti-

Magic Johnson became a figure of considerable sympathy—and controversy—after his dramatic announcement that he had contracted the AIDS virus. (Photo by Brad Mangin)

tudes toward men and women influenced the reaction to Magic. She said, "If it had happened to a heterosexual woman who had been with 100 or 200 men, they'd call her a whore and a slut, and the corporations would drop her like a lead balloon." Martina added, "And she'd never get a job in her life."

Martina also found fault for what she saw as Magic's disregard for women. "What I don't understand is that like, Magic says he was just trying to accommodate these women. That is just terrible. Just think about the word. He's preaching the wrong message. He's saying it's okay to be promiscuous as long as you use a condom. That's not good."

She went on: "It's sad. What does it say for you? Ayn Rand says in her writing you are who you sleep with. Who you surround yourself with, your friends and your lovers. What does it say for these men who hop in bed with a woman every five minutes? It's sad that these women throw themselves in bed, but that doesn't mean he should do that. Be a gentleman. Have some self-respect," she concluded.

Martina's remarks themselves drew a strong reaction—and considerable support from women. "Johnson has not been a hero to women. He has been a hazard," wrote Sally Jenkins. "I do not hear enough concern for his sexual partners, particularly given that AIDS is transmitted far more frequently from males to females than from females to males. I do not hear Johnson admit that he may have done considerable pursuing himself. I do not hear a pronounced enough sense of responsibility." And this, from a male commentator: "Magic has been set up as a hero because of his illness, which is a serious misreading of the facts," says Glenn Dickey. "He is not Lou Gehrig, who fell victim to a disease whose cause is a mystery more than 50 years later. Magic is a man who was victimized by his own self-indulgence, a fault that may have put many women at risk as well."

To his lasting credit, Magic has conceded all the points. He has admitted to reckless sexual behavior with women, while telling everybody who will listen that AIDS is not a "gay disease" but a killer that can strike anybody. He seems, above all, to understand that his actions have had a cost, and yet he accepts this with the grace and equanimity that have characterized his entire life.

Magic Calls It Quits

Martina excepted, a few yahoos came out of the closet with
Magic Johnson's announcement that he had contracted the AIDS
virus. "I don't like people who have AIDS," sniffed Michigan state
legislator Dominic Jacobetti, refusing to support a proclamation in
support of Magic. Equally unfathomable, though far less objec-
tionable, were the statements by Laker teammate A. C. Green that
Magic didn't deserve to play in the 1992 NBA All Star Game. "He's
got to prove he can beat me in practice first," said A. C. Earth to
A. C.: Magic has got *nothing* to prove to you. As Bruce Jenkins said,
asking Magic to prove himself on a basketball court to a guy like
Green is "like telling General MacArthur: 'Forget about that Philip-
pines thing. We want to see you take Fresno.'"

But these comments didn't get to Magic; what finally got to
Magic was when he decided to come back to the NBA for the
1992–93 season after helping the United States win Olympic gold
on the Dream Team. The Olympics were one thing; but coming
back to the NBA scared many people, including one of his fellow
Dream Teamers. "Just because he came back doesn't mean nothing to me," Karl Malone told *The New York Times.* "I'm no fan, no
cheerleader. It may be good for basketball, but you have to look
far beyond that. You have a lot of young men who have a long life
ahead of them. The Dream Team was a concept everybody loved.
But now we're back to reality." Reality was fear. A lot of players—
not just Malone—were afraid that if Magic was cut in a game and
started bleeding, his tainted blood could infect one of them. The
medical community said the chances of this occurring were in-
finitesimal, but the fear among the big men of the NBA persisted
nonetheless.

Then there were other controversies—the whispers that Johnson contracted AIDS not through heterosexual relations as he said,
but through gay sex. It was reported that Isiah Thomas, Magic's
supposed friend, was the person responsible for spreading these
rumors, but they had their spokesmen in the sporting press as well.
"He just wants to play basketball. Fine . . . ," wrote Dave Kindred.
"Now he should do one selfless thing. Tell the whole truth about
how he acquired the AIDS virus. He said unprotected heterosex-

When he wasn't chasing Tim Hardaway around a basketball court, James Worthy could be found scanning the yellow pages looking for interesting things to do. (Photo by Brad Mangin)

ual sex did it. Numbers say that's unlikely. A man is hundreds of times more likely to acquire HIV by homosexual contact or by using dirty hypodermic needles. It is forgivable for a man to hide such activity—if no one else is hurt by his behavior. But it is reprehensible if a man serving his self-interest helps create a frightening lie that causes research money to be diverted from more critical fields."

Swirling like hornets around Magic's imminent return to active NBA life, these controversies and rumors forced him to reconsider his decision and retire permanently. Magic said he loved the game too much to let all this other stuff distract from it. He didn't want to be a sideshow, and he was deeply hurt that many of his onetime peers saw him as a potential menace. Concludes Jack McCallum: "There will always be the reality that Magic, the most popular of players, left the game because some people didn't want him around."

James Worthy's Embarrassment

Basketball fans, like all sports fans, can be cruel sometimes. When police busted Lakers star James Worthy in Houston a few years ago for soliciting prostitutes, did basketball fans sympathize with a lonely ballplayer out on the road perhaps just looking for a little female companionship to help him unwind after a big game? Sure they did.

"I'm still in shock over James Worthy's arrest for soliciting two prostitutes," said one fan. "I thought basketball players were taught to avoid being double teamed." Another speculated that James was just looking for "a pickup game." Yet another fan asked, "Do you suppose Worthy's wife will be waiting for the team when the Lakers return?" Then there were the jokes: "This gives new meaning to the concept of the pregame meal."

Nor is it likely that Worthy ever got any endorsement offers out of this, either. Worthy allegedly called up an "escort service" that he had found in the phone book. The escort service, in fact, was a cover for a police sting operation. But Jan Hubbard, the columnist, thought that James would make a perfect spokesman for the phone company: "Hi, this is James Worthy for the yellow pages . . ."

Taunts

Taunting is an ancient, long-established athletic custom somewhat akin to trash-talkin'. Not only do players do it, but fans can get in on the act, too.

"Welcome to the East, Moe. Tell your troubles to Curly."
>—taunt from Pistons fan to then–Denver Nuggets coach Doug Moe

"Hey, Porter, get a haircut!"
>—Boston fan to the bald Terry Porter (who replied, "Hey, get a team!")

"I hope we see you whores back up here next week."
>—Portland's *Danny Ainge*, ridiculing the Lakers bench after a Trail Blazer thumping of Los Angeles

"Hey, Dawkins, I found your mama's underpants!"
>—*Rick Mahorn*, holding up an extra-large Hefty garbage bag and waving it at Pistons teammate Darryl Dawkins

Gary Payton, taunting Michael Jordan: "Hey, Michael, I've got my millions and I'm buying my Ferraris and Testarossas too!"
Jordan responding: "No problem. I get them for free."

Karl Malone: Dirty Player or Not?

"He's the toughest guy we play because he's the only guy in the league they allow to throw you out of the post. He doesn't just go down and stand there, he goes down there, a guy comes across the middle, and he just throws them out. Nobody else in the league can do that. Maybe because he does it all the time it's perfectly legal, but if we do it, it's a foul. Michael Jordan doesn't score 33 a game throwing people around. He just plays.

"Malone's a great player, but maybe he thinks he's better than he really is. He can score every night, but can he guard people at the other end? It frustrates me that they allow him to do that. Then, instead of playing, he talks trash to coaches on the bench. He should just play basketball. He hasn't won any championships. When he wins some championships and shows me some rings, maybe I can say he's a great player."

—Charlotte coach *Gene Littles*, during the 1990 season

"When things are going well for him, he laughs at all the bumping and shoving. But when things aren't going well and the game is physical, it gets to him. That's when he gets the technicals and gets out of his game. And frankly, I've never seen him pick on anybody his own size."

—anonymous Western Conference coach, as quoted by *Sports Illustrated*

"Barkley is a man. Michael Jordan is a 190-pound man. Karl Malone is not a man . . . you can back him down. That's why I think Utah will never win it with him."

—*Chuck Person*, when he was with Indiana

A Couple of Things Karl Malone Has Said About the Way He Plays the Game

"I make my fouls worth it. But I don't go after anybody. I don't understand these little stabs and jabs that go on from time to time, always when I'm not around. What is a Chuck Person doing in Indiana talking about me? I never said one thing about him. I'd like to think I have more sanity and class than these guys who are always talking about me."

—*Karl Malone*

"If people judged me by what I do on the basketball court, I'd be in jail."

—*Karl Malone*

The Portland Trail Blazers:
Mental Giants, or What?

"Look at their team. They have more athletic ability than we do. But to win, you have to play together as a team and you have to play smart."
—*Michael Jordan*

"You want to force them to make decisions. They're a very athletic team, but when you play against a good, smart team like us, you have to be a smart team, too. No offense to Portland, but we're a much smarter team. They match up against us as well as any team in the league. But our guys play a lot smarter."
—*Scottie Pippen*

"They run the open court so well, we try to get them in a half-court game and make them utilize their minds as much as possible."
—*Michael Jordan*, on the Bulls' strategy when they play the Trail Blazers

"They play stupid. They take all kinds of stupid shots and then they think they can get every rebound. I thought [Danny] Ainge would make them smarter, but he hasn't helped in that way that much, I guess."
—*Michael Jordan*, a few years ago

"They're a lot better than all of us. There is no way any of us should be able to compete with them. But they let us compete. There is no question that they have the best talent. Talent doesn't beat them. Their brains beat them."
—anonymous Western Conference coach, as quoted by Jan Hubbard

"The Portland Trail Blazers couldn't pass the SAT if they all got together and combined their scores."
—remark overheard by basketball fan Jim Larson

Around the NBA: Thoughts, Cheap Shots, Comments

"In the first quarter, he's Clyde the Glide. . . . In the second quarter, he's a guy named Clyde. His shots take on the look of masonry. He misses by miles. He throws bad passes and as always, he dribbles with his head down in the open floor."
>—sportswriter *Bruce Jenkins*, in a critical appraisal of Clyde Drexler

"The trade would have been good for Kevin because restaurants are open later in Detroit."
>—Detroit forward *John Salley*, on a proposed trade that would've brought wide-body Portland center Kevin Duckworth to Detroit

"Let's put it this way. When he was a rookie he didn't have an outside shot, so no one guarded him from 20 feet. Today, still no one guards him from 20 feet."
>—agent *Norm Blass*, on his former client, guard Rod Strickland

"I like the kid, but I wouldn't have given him three—and I don't mean three years. I mean three days."
>—more from *Blass*, on Strickland signing a six-year pact with Portland

"This will be the first time in the history of the league that the referee drops the ball."
>—broadcaster *Dan Issel*, on a jump ball between 5'10" Michael Adams and 5'3" Muggsy Bogues

"Roy Tarpley of the Mavericks fits the description of a player who's available on a 'day to day' basis."
>—*Allan Malamud*, columnist

"It's tough for players like me, who have studied and played the game our whole lives, to have some guy in management who has never played the game telling you what you should be doing. The NBA sure wasn't at all like I thought it was when I was 10 years old and dreaming of being there some day."

> —*Steve Alford*, after being cut by the Dallas Mavericks in 1991

"The money's good, don't get me wrong. But this goes beyond money. They insulted me, they insulted my integrity, me as a person, my character."

> —*Harvey Grant*, during a contract dispute with his club, the Washington Bullets

"In his short career, Anderson has demanded money that exceeded the outrageous, missed all of training camp and already is griping about playing time. Looks like Kenny has the pro game down pat."

> —*Jan Hubbard*, on Kenny Anderson as a rookie

"The Mavericks' Rolando Blackman scored more than the entire Knicks backcourt last week, and he was out injured."

> —*Jan Hubbard*

"An emotional player who may not have the best appreciation of his teammates' strengths and weaknesses. He has yet to establish himself as an unquestioned leader, à la Magic."

> —*Rick Barry*, criticizing Kevin Johnson

"Vlade is like those European soccer players. You ever see one of those guys get tripped? It's like they've been hit with a nine-millimeter cannon."

> —*Kevin Duckworth*, on the "flopping" technique used by Vlade Divac to draw fouls

"Too short, too slow, and too white to make it big in the NBA."

> —*Walt Frazier*, talking about the pro prospects of Cleveland guard Mark Price (the remark, as might be expected, drew considerable fire)

"I think David's a nice player, but he's not worth $26 million."
> —broadcaster *Billy Packer*, when then-rookie David
> Robinson signed his big contract with the Spurs

"Rodney McRae is not a scorer. He looks to shoot when he's on the free-throw line."
> —*Mitch Laurence*, sportswriter

"Karl Malone's basketball trunks are as roomy as jammies. They ought to have Ninja Turtle decals on them."
> —*Mike Downey*, sportswriter

"I don't consider it a big deal because *he's* not a big deal. If this were Lionel Simmons, it would be a major issue. But this is Dennis Hopson."
> —Kings GM *Jerry Reynolds*, after Hopson was slow in
> reporting to the team after being traded there

"Welcome to hell."
> —*Spud Webb*, welcoming Mitch Richmond in the locker
> room after he was traded to the Sacramento Kings

Stops Around the League: A Few NBA Cities

"New York is my kind of town, because I have a gun."
> —*Charles Barkley*

"Portland's image is pretty well captured by its mayor, Bud Clark, a tavern owner who posed as a flasher in a promotion for the local arts community a few years back. The poster showed Mr. Clark, back to the camera, raincoat wide open, flashing a sculpture above the slogan, 'Expose Yourself To Art.' "
> —*Detroit News*, during the 1990 Piston–Trail Blazer
> NBA finals

"Detroit's image is pretty well captured by its mayor, Coleman Young, who recently won reelection after losing a paternity suit.

After being accused of being a malingerer by the Houston Rock-ets management, Hakeem Olajuwon threatened to take his argu-ment with the team to another court—a law court. (Photo courtesy of the Houston Rockets)

When Detroit exposes itself, it's not to art."
> —Portland *Oregonian,* in response to Detroit's jabs

"I didn't understand why people in Seattle continued to harp [on me]. My conclusion is that they're depressed from being rained on all the time."
> —*Dale Ellis*, after being traded from Seattle to Milwaukee

"Coaching in Cleveland is a religious experience. You do a lot of praying, but the answer is usually no."
> —*Bill Fitch*, former Cavaliers coach

"You look at the uniforms we have. They're ugly. We're in Milwaukee. It's cold. It's a place no one really wants to come to. It's easy to have a negative view of Milwaukee and I think it carries over into sports."
> —*Alvin Robertson*, ex–All Star for the Bucks

"The only good thing about San Antonio is the guacamole."
> —*Larry Brown*, former San Antonio coach

Hakeem's Nightmare

So was Hakeem faking it or not? Hakeem Olajuwon, star center for the Houston Rockets, did or did not injure his hamstring late in the 1992 season, depending on whose point of view you take. Houston general manager Steve Patterson took a hard line, implying that Hakeem did not have an injury and suspending him from the team. In response, Hakeem blew a cork. "He has attacked my reputation, my integrity," said Hakeem, who demanded an apology and asked to be traded. "Tell Steve he's stupid, I'll sue them for everything they've got."

But Patterson and the Rockets pointed out that Olajuwon was given a clean bill of health by a doctor, but still refused to play. This did not soothe Hakeem the Dream's ruffled feelings at all. "I don't expect any apology because you are not dealing with classy people here," he said. "Charlie [Thomas, Rockets owner] has been a coward standing behind the organization. So Steve Patterson is not even worth talking about." Later Hakeem decided to take his own advice and not make any more comments on the matter: "In my country of Nigeria, we have a saying: 'It's best to be silent when dealing with fools.'"

Rick Reilly agreed with Olajuwon. "Am I reading this right?" he wrote in *Sports Illustrated.* "For his whole career, this team has thrown Mr. Olajuwon deadbeats and doorknobs for teammates. Guys like Ralph Sampson, Joe Barry Carroll and Sleepy Floyd. He has been an All Star six times, and he has usually played with four guys who looked as if they were on their lunch break at the Y. So one time he tells management his hamstring hurts and he can't play, and you don't believe him? This man is honorable. He wants an apology. Apologize." The Rockets management did not listen to Reilly any more than they did to Olajuwon.

Patrick Grumbles

"You don't go to the press and tell them Patrick's getting too many shots. Tell me to my face, or tell them to go to management and tell them to trade me. Then we'll see who's going to go. The person or persons who said it are very immature, but unfortunately that's the type of players we have on this ballclub."

> —*Patrick Ewing*, after some of his Knicks teammates criticized him anonymously for taking too many shots and caring more about making the All Star team than winning

Grumbles About Patrick

"A few things to know about Patrick Ewing: Outside of last year's [1990] playoffs, when the Knicks eliminated the Celtics in Boston, he's never shown a trace of championship-style leadership."
> —*Bruce Jenkins*, sportswriter

"Assuming the mind of the sporting public has not lost its capacity to be boggled, Patrick Ewing's refusal a couple of weeks ago to accept the New York Knicks' contract offer of $33 million over six years, well, boggles the mind. The contract would have made

Ewing the highest-paid athlete in the history of team sports. Ewing's one-two counterpunch—spurning the deal and requesting that an arbitrator decide if he can become a free agent before this season—appears to be an act of phenomenal greed."
    —*Jack McCallum*, 1991

"Patrick Ewing longs for 'freedom,' which comes as a surprise to many people in the New York area who thought he really only lusted for money. . . . Ewing may be a great center but he is also the prototypical selfish athlete. Business comes first, winning comes second. The Ewing arbitration is about nothing more than money. And his cries for freedom are nothing short of repugnant."
    —*Jan Hubbard*

"Ewing did more bitching than Leona Helmsley, demanded more money than Ivana Trump, and was as effective a leader as David Dinkins."
    —*Rotisserie League Basketball,* summing up Ewing's
        1990–91 season

Another Big Guy with an Attitude

James Donaldson, said Derek Harper, is a "seven-foot punk." Harper said this after Donaldson got into a tussle during practice with one of their teammates on the Mavericks, Rolando Blackman. The team suspended Donaldson for one game for this transgression, which the big center thought was grossly unfair: "This is the biggest joke I've ever been involved in in my life," he said. "It is totally ludicrous, unjust and ridiculous, too."

Another story about Big Bad Jim would seem to confirm the Harper observation. One year Mavericks backup center John Shasky hit Donaldson during a practice scrimmage. Donaldson was furious and vowed revenge—"even if it takes 10 years."

A week later, as the team was leaving the floor after practice, Donaldson nailed Shasky with a right hand that put him on the ground. Shasky felt he'd been sucker-punched, but Donaldson told him he should feel grateful. "Because you didn't have to wait 10 years," he explained.

When It Comes to Attitude, a Guy Who Could Teach Both Ewing and Donaldson a Thing or Two

"His face takes on the look of a spoiled child after dessert."
—sportswriter *Dan Shaughnessy*, on how Danny Ainge looks after being called for a foul

"Actually, I'm not a complainer. I'm a whiner."
—*Danny Ainge*, clarifying things

"He is still a fine white whine, but no longer improving with age."
—*Rotisserie League Basketball,* on Ainge as he grows older

"Danny Ainge couldn't play shortstop, second base, third base, or the outfield, hit a jump shot, or guard Andrew Toney."
—joke about Ainge, circa 1984, after he failed in his attempt to become a professional baseball player

"Ainge hurt his back picking up a suitcase. It must have had his contract in it."
—*Dick Motta*, on a Danny Ainge injury when he was playing for Sacramento

What Earl Strom Thinks of Darrell Garretson

It's hard to sympathize with guys like Danny Ainge and Mark Aguirre, who whine like stuck pigs after they're called for a foul. But if you listen to former referee Earl Strom talk about the quality of the officiating in the NBA, maybe the whiners have a point. After retiring in 1990 after five decades as an NBA official, Earl Strom wrote a book in which he blasted the league's supervisor of officials, Darrell Garretson, for being dictatorial, tyrannical, and, in short, a real meanie. Tell us about it, Earl:

"They just want refs who are just going to follow The System, Garretson's beloved guidelines for where you're supposed to be and how you're supposed to stand, and never mind developing the judg-

ment and command. Everything is planned, diagrammed and ruled to death."

"I think he wants to be the second coming of [legendary referee] Mendy Rudolph. That's not in the cards. His personality doesn't lend itself to that. He's a very immature person. He has a lot of hangups. He keeps looking for an identity. I keep hoping he'll find it someday."

"I see guys trying to upstage each other out on the court. The feelings of the pro-Garretson refs and the anti-Garretson refs are so strong that one guy will make a call at one end, and the other guy will say, 'I'll get that s.o.b.,' and make a call that upstages him at the other end."

"He sets himself up as the last word. Well, he isn't the last word. He's insensitive, he dehumanizes people and he's vindictive enough to never forget an incident where there was a disagreement between him and another referee. The league has taken the attitude that if it ain't broke, don't fix it. Well, it is broke. It just hasn't been exposed."

Say, Earl, Has Darrell Ever Tried to Rebut Any of the Terrible Things You've Said About Him?

"Garretson's made a few remarks to other people, but not directly to me, about how I failed as a referee and how I will fail as a TV commentator. If I failed as a referee, he may be the only one who knows it."

—*Earl Strom*

The Best Comeback We Ever Heard by a Referee Who'd Just Been Insulted

Since we're talking about (and insulting) refs, let's give equal time. The honor of Best Insult by a Referee Who'd Just Endured a Verbal Tongue-Lashing During a Game belongs to NBA ref Joey Crawford. According to Steve Tady, who told us this story, Golden State Warriors team physician Robert Albo was jumping all over Crawford

during a game, telling him how terrible he was and what a stinker of a game he was calling. Besides being the team doctor, Albo is a rabid fan who sits at courtside and normally just buries the referees under a mountain of invective. Finally, Crawford could take no more. As he was walking over to the scorer's table being pursued by a steady stream of ridicule from Albo, the referee turned and said calmly, "Hey doc, at least I don't bury my mistakes." That shut Albo up.

Basketball Owners, General Managers, and Other Executive Types of Questionable Value

Idle chatter by and about some of the men who occupy the front offices and executive suites of the NBA:

"If he doesn't take that job, he's crazy. Coaches get fired every day, but a GM can be dumb and last forever."
> —*Doug Moe*, on whether one of his assistants should try for a coaching job or take a general manager's job that had been offered him

"I never had a relationship with Al when I was the coach. I don't have a relationship with Al now, and I won't have a relationship with Al down the road."
> —former Knicks coach *Rick Pitino*, on his relationship with Knicks GM Al Bianchi

"I think you made a big mistake, and judging by your record as a general manager, it's not your first."
> —marketing executive *Mike Ornstein* to Cleveland's Wayne Embry, after Embry and others on the Olympic selection committee did not pick Isiah Thomas for the Dream Team

"You're the worst f—— GM in the league!"
> —Knicks executive *Dave Checketts* to Dallas GM Rick Sund, after Sund turned down a trade deal offered by Checketts at the 1992 college draft

"Note to David Stern: Yo, commish, doesn't Clippers general manager Elgin Baylor deserve a gold chair in recognition of his long and meritorious service in the draft lottery?"

—*Inside Sports* magazine, ridiculing Baylor and the Clippers for their string of bad draft picks

"I played Jerry like an accordion."

—rookie *Jayson Williams*, mocking Jerry Colangelo after starting a feud with the Phoenix executive and forcing a trade to Philadelphia

"He treated me the same way he treated everybody else—rude, obnoxious, and uncaring. If they think they did him any harm by firing him, they're dead wrong. I'm sure they thought they humiliated Bill by firing him and putting blame on him. But Bill didn't want that job to begin with. So the owner did him a favor. Now he can get paid and still tee off on time."

—*Derek Smith*, a former Sacramento Kings player, after NBA legend Bill Russell was fired as a Kings executive in 1990

"This is not to sound prejudiced, but half the squad should be white. I think people are afraid to speak out on that subject. White people have to have white heroes. I'll be truthful. I respect them [blacks], but I need white people. It's in me."

—*Ted Stepien*, when he was owner of the Cleveland Cavaliers in the early 1980s

"We were expecting it. We're also expecting him to name himself as coach of the Hornets next year and to name himself the starting center."

—a member of the Charlotte Coliseum governing board, after Hornets owner George Shinn demanded to renegotiate his lease in 1990 to get more money

"I don't want to hear another word about David Stern. The savior of the NBA. Made it popular again. Deserves the $27.5 million deal. Right. And if Wolf Blitzer had the job as Stern did, at the same time Magic and Bird were hitting their strides, we'd be saying the same thing about him."

—*Rick Reilly*, sportswriter

"Earth to the NBA and Commissioner David Stern. Please drop your inaccurate 'banned for life' phrase for three-time drug offenders. The correct phrase is that they are 'banned for a minimum of two years.' Anytime a player is banned for life, it is a contradiction if he is allowed to return after two years."

—*Jan Hubbard*, on Michael Wiggins's reinstatement in 1989 after supposedly being banned for life by the NBA for drug violations

Draft Talk

Abrasive comments, unkind speculations, and rude remarks from NBA drafts of years past:

"The Sonics need a center in the worst way, and Shintzius is a center in the worst way."

—columnist *Steve Kelley*, on the prospect of drafting University of Florida center Dwayne Schintzius

"Chicago simply wasted their pick. The perfect guy would have been Rodney Monroe, a guard who can really shoot. That way, they could get rid of Dennis Hopson and Craig Hodges and not think twice. Instead, they get a 6'9" guy [Kansas forward Mark Randall] whose potential is suspect. What did they do, draft him so he could room with Will Perdue?"

—sportswriter *Bruce Jenkins*, on the 1991 draft

"Where's he going to go? You can't shoot 15-foot airballs in the NBA."

—then–UNLV coach *Jerry Tarkanian*, scoffing at reports that Stacey Augmon would leave the school as a junior and enter the pros

"I knew it would happen. Whoever told him to go hardship ought to be shot. He needed to play point guard here. If he was here, he'd be All-American, he'd be one of the top three guards in college, and we'd be a Top Ten team."

> —*Jerry Tarkanian*, after one of his former players, Anderson Hunt, was cut by the Celtics in 1991 (Hunt chose to skip his senior year at UNLV and turn pro as a free agent)

"We're ready to pull the trigger but nobody wants to do anything. I can't find anybody to talk to. If I can't do it, it can't be done. I can't even get a counterproposal from anyone."

> —Warriors coach *Don Nelson*, complaining about the dearth of trade activity prior to the 1991 draft

"Let's face it, we all screwed up on Mutombo by letting him slide to number four. But what Nellie is saying, that we wanted Richmond and both number-ones, is his way of saving face. We only wanted one of the two firsts and Richmond. And we would have taken either one. Nelson just doesn't want anyone to realize he screwed up, too."

> —Kings GM *Jerry Reynolds*, on Don Nelson's claims that the reason he didn't pick Dikembe Mutombo in the draft was that Sacramento was demanding too high a price in return

"Take the Clippers' draft—please. Everyone in basketball knew that the Clips had to vastly improve their leadership at the point position and get some more physical players up front. So, *Randy Woods?* How is a nasty 5'11" gunner, a guy who only passes the ball if you hold an Uzi to his head, going to help? . . . How much longer will we have to wait for this franchise to become even above average? Will we live to see it? Will our children?"

> —*Tom Kertes*, sportswriter, after the Clippers' 1992 draft

Players We Have Known (Old-Timer's Division)

"In December of [1987], Chris Washburn was traded to Atlanta for the rights to Ken Barlow. Barlow was playing in Europe at the time. He was small, slow and had no chance of playing in the NBA. He was just a name so the transaction would be official. The Warriors had traded the third pick of the [1986] draft to Atlanta for nothing. They got a bargain."

> —*C. W. Nevius*, on one of the biggest washouts in NBA history, Chris Washburn

"Have an oversized flamingo and a pterodactyl ever thrown elbows at each other while wearing short pants? That's what the sight looks like."

> —*Larry Merchant*, watching gawky Lakers seven-footer Mel Counts tangle under the backboards with gangly 6'8" forward Phil Jackson of the Knicks in the early 1970s

"McAdoo, McAdon't, McAwill, McAwon't."

> —joking rhyme about the on-again, off-again moods of the high-scoring Bob McAdoo

"Hey, when I looked over, you was winning."

> —*Dick Barnett,* when asked by Don Nelson why he hadn't helped him when Nelson had gotten into a fight during a game

"The ball looks as if it belongs on the nose of a seal."

> —comment about the red, white, and blue ball of the now-defunct ABA

"Funk is not a bad word. Funk is being jazzy. As a matter of fact, there are two kinds of funk: Jazzy Funk and Funk Beyond Control. I am the only person who has ever harnessed Funk Beyond Control and that's why only I have Close Encounters of the Funkiest Kind."

> —*Darryl Dawkins*, on his funky self

"The biggest waste of space since Greenland."
— remark about Dawkins toward the end of his career

Around the NBA (II)

"Who would you have vote instead? Writers? They're fucking idiots. Coaches? They're fucking idiots. Trainers . . . now that would be a good idea."
— *Doug Moe*, after the fans voted A. C. Green onto the 1990 All Star starting lineup

"There's no down side to the trade. If he doesn't play, I'll waive his butt."
— Denver coach *Doug Moe*, after the Nuggets acquired the lackadaisical Joe Barry Carroll in a 1990 trade

"A lot of times you don't see things clearly until they happen, and then it's too late. Take Darryl Dawkins. Everybody thought he had so much potential, and they waited and waited for him to develop and finally, once he got traded, he got traded a lot. J. R. can be that, too. He can play for a lot of coaches before his career is over."
— *Gene Littles*, Charlotte Hornets coach

"If Chuck Person didn't mouth off, who would know who he is?"
— *Red Auerbach,* on the mouthy star of the Minnesota Timberwolves

"Benoit Benjamin isn't just an underachieving basketball player. He is a symbol for all athletes who don't care enough to do their best. He is a poster boy for sloth. He is a man in constant search of a hammock."
— sportswriter *Michael Ventre,* on the journeyman center

"Sometimes it takes a year, à la Tyrone Hill. Sometimes it happens right away, à la Richmond and Hardaway. Sometimes it never happens, à la Tellis Frank."
— Warriors coach *Don Nelson*, discussing how young players fare in the NBA

"It's not a hard series to figure. It's as simple as David and Goliath. It's big versus small and small versus big, and you probably know how that turned out. Every now and then David slew Goliath, but not many times. They don't record how many times Goliath kicked the shit out of David."

> —*Don Nelson*, assessing the 1991 playoffs between (small) Golden State and (big) San Antonio (in this case, the little guys whipped Goliath)

"I call him the Don Nelson of agents: He always sees how far he can go with the rules without breaking them."

> —ex–NBA star *John Lucas*, on player agent David Falk

"When you play for the Clippers, you feel like you're coming over on one of those boats from Cuba with all different kinds of people on it."

> —*Darnell Valentine*, on playing for the shipwrecked Los Angeles Clippers in the mid-1980s

"Last night and tonight will go down in history. That's a guy who got punched out in the CBA, so they let him come to the big leagues. I had thoughts of rage. Clearly, the good refs took the night off."

> —*Dick Motta*, complaining about NBA referee Pete Quinn, a former CBA ref who was once punched by a player

"Calls came from everywhere. Media people called, some people from rest homes called. They sound about the same."

> —Lakers coach *Mike Dunleavy*, on receiving numerous calls of advice after the Bulls whipped Los Angeles in the 1991 finals

"Ken Calvert must have overdosed on FM radio as a teenager. He is so insufferably in love with the sound of his voice that you constantly want to cuff him one upside the ear. Each time James Edwards scores, this guy's 'Buuuuuuudha!' gets a little longer—almost

stretching into the next basket. When the Pistons finally dump him, he'll have to spin records at wedding receptions."
—sportswriter *Rick Bonnell*, on the voice of the Pistons

"Shut the fuck up and play!"
—*Xavier McDaniel* to Scottie Pippen, after Pippen complained to the refs about rough play by the Knicks in the brutal 1992 New York–Chicago playoff series

Basketball Insult Nicknames

Most sports fans tend to associate colorful nicknames with baseball, but basketball does pretty well in this regard too. One of my favorites is Sports Illustrated, the name they gave to Charles Shackleford of the 76ers. The reason? He only plays once a week. Here are some other good ones:

Airball One

The nickname for the charter jet used by the Sacramento Kings, one of the NBA's worst road teams.

Al Batross

New York Knick general manager Al Bianchi, so dubbed by Knicks fans for repeated personnel blunders that have helped drag the team down.

Alton Listless

Seven-foot Alton Lister has, at times over his career, lacked for what the French—those great fans of the hoop game—call joie de vivre. Hence, the sobriquet.

Animal

"Forward Kenny Gattison is nicknamed Animal," writes George Shirk, "which would be okay if that animal knew how to play basketball."

Blunderburke

Irate Hoosier fans hung this tag on Lawrence Funderburke after the talented 6'9" forward transferred from Indiana University to Ohio State following disagreements with coach Bobby Knight. "Nobody talks about the good things in my life," said Funderburke, in response to the badgering he's received from Indiana supporters.

"I make good grades. I help kids. I go to class. I don't do drugs. Yet everyone chastises me for a sport that's basically a diversion. Basketball is just a dream world."

Basketball a dream world? Obviously, this kid wasn't cut out to play for Bobby Knight.

Brainlock

Rotisserie League Basketball thinks that instead of Mookie Blaylock, it should be "Mookie Brainlock."

Chalk

Manute Bol's name for his buddy, the very white Chris Mullin. Mullin is also known as Casper—as in the Friendly Ghost—or, in Rick Reilly's phrase, "the Man the Sun Forgot."

Charmin' Armon

Armon Gilliam earned this monicker because he's so *soft* under the boards.

Cheeseburger, Whale, Porky, Fat Boy, the Big O

The large and rotund Oliver Miller—his weight can balloon up to 335 pounds—has been called all these names by fans, but he purports not to care. "When they ask me if I want a cheeseburger, I tell them, 'Sure. Just hold the onions and cut the mayo and pickles.'"

Chicken with Stars

This was the tag they hung on Tony Campbell when he played in Los Angeles. The Laker firmament was full of stars on and off the court, and Campbell was a rather tentative reserve who seemed a little overwhelmed by it all at times. Tony's fortunes improved considerably after he left the Lakers.

Coupon Clippers

Derogatory term for the Los Angeles Clippers, because of their cut-rate brand of basketball. The team was once known as "the Flippers" because, when they played in San Diego, their arena was located near Sea World.

Crumbs

Michael Jordan has quarreled often with Bulls general manager Jerry Krause, and so came up with this nickname for him. "He always had doughnut crumbs on his lapel," explains M.J.

Dinner Bell Turpin

When he was at Kentucky, Mel Turpin never missed a meal, so coach Joe B. Hall assigned a student to stick with the 6'11" 255-pounder at all times to make sure he didn't overindulge.

Fat Flight

At Arkansas, as the 6'9", 300-plus-pound Oliver Miller graduated, they made room at the dinner table for his replacement at center, 6'9", 320-pound Dwight "Fat Flight" Stewart.

Fennis the Menace

Fennis Dembo, formerly of the University of Wyoming, was an Armour-quality ham. Before going on the road to play UTEP (El Paso) and Brigham Young, he said, "We've got to go down there and sweep both of them. We're going to do it and you can put it in your newspapers so that they can read it." They did, and the Cowboys lost both games. But Fennis was unconquerable. With Fennis sitting on the rim leading the hometown faithful in cheers after the Cowboys clinched a berth in the 1986 NIT, his coach, Rick Dees, assessed him this way: "Fennis has a great personality and is a fine person. Ah, let's face it. He's a hot dog."

Great White Hype

Phrasemaker Charles Barkley's term for Danny Ferry, the pro bust from Duke. *Rotisserie League Basketball* sums Ferry up perfectly: "We were misquoted. We never said he'd be the second coming of Magic Johnson. We said he would be the second coming of Lady Bird Johnson and, given his performance, we feel vindicated."

Hot Plate Williams

There are two players named John Williams in the NBA. One John Williams is known as "Hot Rod" and plays for Cleveland. The other John Williams is known by the nicknames Hot Plate, Hot

Bristlehead (Chris Mullin) meets the Human Solar Eclipse (Mark Eaton) in a standoff under the basket. (Photo by Brad Mangin)

Fudge, and Hot Cross Buns, and he plays for anybody who'll have him.

House
The nickname for Cliff Levingston, who has thrown up so many bricks in his career he could build one.

The Human Injured List, Mr. Rehab, Man of a Thousand Stitches
Nicknames for the oft-injured Denver guard Todd Lichti.

Human Solar Eclipse
Who else but Mark Eaton, the 7'4" Herman Munster lookalike for the Utah Jazz. Disparaging remarks about Eaton abound. When Jeff Ruland returned to the 76ers in 1992 after knee surgery, he made his comeback debut against Hakeem Olajuwon and the Houston Rockets. "Instead of Hakeem, I would have preferred it would

have been against a big slug like Eaton," he said. The news that Eaton had injured himself while jumping in a game brought this comment from Bob Ford: "Now, why would he go and try that after all these years?"

Inaction Jackson

The wits over at *Rotisserie League Basketball* love to pick on Mark Jackson. They wrote that "Inaction Jackson was suspended for two games last season after declaring that the game wasn't fun anymore. He should see it from where we sit." Then, when the 35-year-old Maurice Cheeks came to play for the Knicks, they added, "Just when the migraines were starting to clear up, along comes the opportunity to play alongside Mark Jackson. Can't we, as a nation, take better care of our elderly?"

The Incredible Sulk

What some people are calling the gifted but moody star of the New Jersey Nets, Derrick Coleman.

Joe Barely Cares

And Joe Barry Carroll barely does. With the Warriors playing the Lakers in a 1987 playoff game, fiery Golden State coach George Karl was desperately trying to push his team to an upset win. "Just relax and enjoy," Joe Barry told him. "We can't beat the Lakers." (Similarly, another laid-back NBA center, Benoit Benjamin, once told a disappointed teammate after a hard loss, "Hey, you've got to learn to be more casual.")

Legs 'n' Butt

This was Dennis Scott's nickname in high school, even before he arrived at Georgia Tech. Another player with a rather large derriere is pro Rick Mahorn, the one-time Detroit Piston Bad Boy. An earthquake hit southern California one year when the team was in Los Angeles to play the Lakers, but Vinnie Johnson in his hotel room mistook it for something else. "I thought that quake was just Mahorn on the floor above me—shaking his big fat ass."

Long and Wrong

Charles Barkley's name for David Robinson's golf game.

Lucadaisical

Not exactly awe-inspiring since becoming a pro, Australian-born Luc Longley nevertheless has his allies. Andrew Vlahov, a mainstay on Stanford's 1991 NIT championship team, watched Longley score 20 points for Minnesota in a game and wrote, "The Timberwolves lost again, but Luc's performance was the highlight of the night. . . . The interesting thing was why he played so little. The coach, Jimmy Rodgers, is either blind or doesn't like Luc. Luc was by far the most productive of the three 7-footers on the team. The team's starter, Felton Spencer, managed six points and less rebounds in about 32 minutes of play. A dismal performance." It may or may not be relevant that Vlahov is a fellow Australian and was writing for an Australian newspaper.

Mean Larry Smith

A conversation between a reporter and Larry Smith on how he got his nickname:

Smith: "It goes back to college. A long time ago. It happened, and the name stuck with me."

Reporter: "What happened?"

Smith: "I'm not really at liberty to say. But overall, I think I'm a pretty good person."

McFilthy and McNasty

What they used to call rough and tough board men Jeff Ruland and Rick Mahorn, when they played together for the Bullets in the 1980s. "Truly the bad boys of the eighties," says Jan Hubbard. Now paired with Charles Barkley of the 76ers, the aging Mahorn has been dubbed "the Ground Round of Rebound" by one sportswriter.

The Mouth That Roared

Writer Jack McCallum's name for Indiana's hot-shooting and hot-talking Chuck Person.

Miami Sleet

Their shooting was so cold one year that they weren't the Heat, they were the Sleet.

Old Mount Baldy

"On top of Old Baldy, all covered with snow . . ." Kareem Abdul-Jabbar, toward the end of his career. In his farewell tour of the league, many wits also referred to him as "the rolling grandfather."

Pit

His teammates on the Celtics called Kevin Stacom "Pit" because he used to sweat so much and, it is presumed, smell so bad.

Prince of Darkness, His Heinous, the Consummate Provocateur, Ax Murderer

Nicknames for—who else?—Bill Laimbeer.

Rigor Artis

Sportswriter Peter May's name for the cement-shoed Artis Gilmore, late in his career.

Round Mound of Rebound, Etc.

When Charles Barkley was at Auburn, he had a weight problem. His favorite food was pizza, and students at opposing schools used to throw pizzas at him and wave pizzas suggestively from the stands. In at least one case, they had a pizza delivered to him while he was sitting on the bench during a game. Students also poked fun at him with names like Love Boat, Food World, Runaway Bread Truck, Amana (after the refrigerator maker, get it?), Doughboy, Porky Pig on a Trampoline, Fathead, Fatboy, Crisco Kid, Boy Gorge, Leaning Tower of Pizza, Goodtime Blimp, Tons of Fun, and, of course, the more complimentary one that followed him into the pros, the Round Mound of Rebound. The writer Jeff Coplon also coined a good one about Charles: "The Square Bear of Midair."

Stanley "Call Me Anthing, Just Don't Call Me Late for Supper" Roberts

From *The Sporting News* and not really a nickname, but it sure fits the case.

George Shinnbrenner

The name they've given the meddling pipsqueak owner of the

Charlotte Hornets, George Shinn. Unhappy Charlotte fans also have a saying about him: "Shinn Happens."

Stiff, Dog, No-Hoper

These sobriquets do not apply to any specific individuals; rather, it is how Doug Moe divides up the lower echelon of players in the NBA. Explains Moe: "A stiff is a guy without much talent but who helps you win games. A guy without much talent who doesn't is a dog. A no-hoper is a guy who's not quite good enough to be a stiff yet."

Tidy Bol

An unflattering nickname for Manute Bol, as his game has deteriorated over the years. Other somewhat more complimentary names for him: the Dinka Dunker, the Human Exclamation Mark, the "Human Yardstick" (coined by Jack McCallum). When Manute came to play in Oakland for the Warriors, one local magazine dubbed him "Best New Highrise."

The Typographical Error

Old-time ABA player Wes Bialosuknia, for obvious reasons.

Wilt the Stilt:
A Short Chapter on a Big Guy

Two decades after he retired from the NBA, Wilt Chamberlain is still a legend. The greatest offensive player in the history of the game, his achievements and his equally commanding personality continue to attract attention. How could such a great scorer be such a crummy foul shooter? If he was so great, why didn't his teams win more championships? Are his phenomenal scoring records—on the court and off—legitimate? Just as they were when he was a schoolboy wonder at Overbrook High in Philly, people are still talking about the Stilt.

Over the Years with Wilt

"If I had to pick a single word to describe Wilt, it would be suspicious."

—sportswriter, on the young Wilt Chamberlain

"I've given up on him. He wants the whole world. Whatever school gets him is gonna have to give him a new car, a few thousand dollars, and a house for his parents. That's what he wants. He's a greedy kid."

—college recruiter, trying to woo Chamberlain when he was in high school

"I feel sorry for the Stilt. When he enters the NBA four years from now, he'll have to take a cut in salary."

—sportswriter *Len Lewin*, after Chamberlain decided to attend the University of Kansas amid rumors of hefty under-the-table payments

"It was a pleasure meeting you, but I don't believe a word you said."

— NCAA investigator, after interviewing Chamberlain over alleged improprieties by Kansas in his recruiting

"Wilt Chamberlain was pampered, not picked on. Sure he was belted, but everybody gets belted in the NBA. Without basketball, Wilt Chamberlain would become just another big man."

— 76ers coach *Dolph Schayes*, after Chamberlain complained of rough treatment when he entered the pros

"He's not a good basketball player, simply a big basketball player."

— *Dick Young*, sportswriter

"Any high school kid can do better than that, and this guy is a pro making several thousands of dollars. All he has to do is practice a little. If he practices 100 shots a day for a month, he'd be twice as good as he is. He obviously has no confidence."

— *Dolph Schayes*, on Wilt's spectacularly bad foul shooting (to critics of his foul shooting, Wilt responded: "They don't pay me to make free throws")

"Wilt copped out in the last game. Any injury short of a broken leg or a broken back isn't good enough. When he took himself out of that game, when he hurt his knee, well, I wouldn't have put him back in the game either."

— Celtics center *Bill Russell*, after Wilt took himself out of the seventh game of the 1969 championship series complaining of a bad knee (Wilt later asked to return, but Lakers coach Butch van Breda Kolff refused, and Los Angeles lost the game and the series to Russell's Celtics)

"What it's all about is winning and losing, and he has done a lot of losing."

— *Bill Russell*

Jim Murray, on Wilt the Stilt

Being over seven feet tall is unusual at any time, but back in Chamberlain's time, it was *very* unusual. Here are some lines by Pulitzer prize–winning sportswriter Jim Murray joking about the 7'1" "giant":

"He was put together in a laboratory by a mad doctor with a pair of pliers, a screwdriver and a Bunsen burner. If you look at Chamberlain, you can see the bolts in the forehead. You don't feed it, you oil it, baby."

"Even in summer, Wilt has snow on top. If he ever gets tired of basketball, he could rent himself out as a community antenna. To rush him to the doctor, you'd need a hook and ladder."

"Sir Edmund Hillary was introduced to Wilt, and promptly organized an expedition to climb it . . ."

And, after Murray visited Chamberlain's hilltop mansion in the hills of Los Angeles:

"It's not a house, it's a nursery rhyme in brick. The lord of the house should go around saying, 'Fe, fi, fo, fum!' It's the kind of place you'd expect to see a lot of little kids in mouse hats riding plastic elephants. The rooms are South American batcave."

Wilt Encounters a Fan

Like Bill Russell, Kareem Abdul-Jabbar, and other big men, Wilt has had an uneasy relationship with the much shorter public. One time, according to legend, a fan came up to Wilt and asked, "How's the weather up there?" But if you're a fan and you're going to make a stupid joke like that to a big man, you'd better make sure that the big man is in a good mood that day. As it happened, Wilt was not in a good mood, and he answered, "Raining," and spit on him.

Wilt Sounds Off

Besides his obviously commanding physical presence, one of the reasons that Wilt continues to cause comment even today is that he often says interesting things. Ego-driven, yes. Obnoxious, sometimes. But usually interesting. A sampling of the tall man's opinions:

On the mentality of NBA owners: "There are too many whites who get a vicarious thrill from being in control of players. They are willing to pay too much money for a team in order to say, 'Michael Jordan plays for me.' If a black guy wants to rub shoulders with Jordan, he just goes to the disco. The white guys buy him."

On Celtics boss Red Auerbach: "I don't like Auerbach. He coached five blacks and he had insights about playing them. But he didn't have anything to do with getting them. That was done by the old owner, Walter Brown. Brown was the guy who said it was okay to have blacks on a team in Boston."

On Pat Riley departing as Lakers coach: "I think Pat was actually fired. I know firsthand from people who would know these things that Pat was not quite the guy who many in the Lakers organization wanted him to be. He became too hard a taskmaster and he became bigger than his job. . . . The people he worked with, for and around didn't want him around anymore. It's too bad because I remember Pat, from the days we played together on the Lakers, as a good man. It's strange what power can do. In Pat's case, it seemed like it went straight to his head."

On a previous Lakers coach, Butch van Breda Kolff, whom Chamberlain played for: "Van Breda Kolff may have known a little more about coaching basketball from a technical standpoint, but he was so ignorant of basic human relations that he was an utterly hopeless coach."

On Kareem Abdul-Jabbar: "No heart. That's why he never played in the streets anywhere. He never played in the Rucker tournament."

On playing against Kareem: "I had experience and strength going for me against Kareem. I also had an intangible—the gut-it-out toughness I'd picked up playing schoolyard ball as a kid. Kareem had never done that, and it's hurt his game—as great as he is."

Wilt and Kareem

What is it about these legendary NBA centers anyway? Bill Russell takes pot shots at Wilt, and vice versa. And you definitely do not want to invite Wilt and Kareem Abdul-Jabbar to the same cocktail party. Not only would it be extremely difficult to find furniture they could sit in comfortably, the two do not get along. *At all.*

According to Wilt, their antipathy dates back to the late sixties, after Kareem (then Lew Alcindor) left New York to begin his great career at UCLA. When Kareem was at Power Memorial High School in New York and Wilt was a star in the pros, the duo sometimes hung together. Played some ball, went down to Greenwich Village, rapped. Wilt even gave advice and counseling to the shy young kid who was the most highly sought after high school basketball recruit since, well, Wilt Chamberlain. But after Lew blew town and became Kareem, their friendship fell apart, says Wilt.

This was Wilt talking when he was still playing for the Lakers and Kareem was on the Milwaukee Bucks: "When he got to UCLA and then turned pro and got so heavily into the black pride/black power thing, he started to snub me. He seems to think that because I haven't changed my name and still have a lot of white friends, I've abandoned the black man. Hell, he hardly even talks to me anymore. He won't even look at me when the Lakers play the Bucks and we jump center."

Of course, Wilt failed to mention that he has fanned the flames over the years with a series of statements denigrating Abdul-Jabbar's abilities. Many people think that Wilt is simply jealous over Kareem being talked about as the greatest center of all time—even better than a certain 7'1" somebody with a goatee and a mansion in the Los Angeles hills.

The more reserved Abdul-Jabbar finally spoke up for himself when he published his autobiography a few years ago. In "an open letter to Wilt Chumperlane," he accuses Wilt of "jealousy and envy" of Kareem's many titles in the pros and college. And like Bill Russell, he attacked Chamberlain for wimping out in that 1969 championship game in which the Celtics beat the Lakers by two points and claimed the world title. "After any tough test in which you didn't do well, you blamed those around you and quit," Kareem writes. "Your professional career was marked by the same kind of pattern. In professional basketball, Bill Russell and the Boston Celtics gave you a yearly lesson in real competitive competence and teamwork. All you could say was that your teammates stunk and that you had done all you could and besides, the refs never gave you a break. Poor Wilt."

After complaining for years about how he always got stuck with a losing team, Wilt "came out to L.A. and got with a dream team," Kareem continues. "The only lack that team had was leadership at the center position." Kareem concludes, "People will remember that I worked with my teammates and helped us win. You will be remembered as a whining crybaby and a quitter, stats and all."

After the book came out, somebody asked Wilt for his reply and he referred reporters to his sister. "My sister asked me if she could go knock him out," Wilt said.

20,000

Some expressed amazement and awe. Others expressed disdain and skepticism. Still others, comedians in particular, reacted with wit and humor to Wilt's claims about his greatest achievement—that over his lifetime, he had slept with 20,000 women.

"There will be an I-Slept-with-Wilt-Chamberlain reunion—at Madison Square Garden. Twenty thousand women? What was his best pickup line—'Next'?"
—*Bob Sarlatte*

"Wilt Chamberlain says his New Year's resolution is to stop fooling around so much. He wants to find the right 200 or 300 women and settle down."
—*Jay Leno*

"Thank you for standing in line tonight. I don't know what it is, but saying that made me feel like Wilt Chamberlain."
— *David Letterman*, welcoming the audience to a "Late Night" anniversary show

"I still love basketball, but recent revelations in that sport have compelled me to update the stately wedding formula of yesteryear. I no longer ask the groom: 'Wilt thou take this woman?' "
— *Rev. Henry Hall*, as told to Glenn Dickey

"Let's see, that comes to 2,168 cases of Riunite, 881 crates of Trojan Magnums, and one very well worn Barry White album."
— *Esquire* magazine, speculating on what Chamberlain might have used during his quest

"We're not sure what it means, but we still think somebody is lying. When we do the arithmetic, Wilt's time in Philadelphia should have produced about 5,000 calls on the yes line."
— *Philadelphia Daily News*, after receiving only 1,978 yes calls to a phone poll of Philadelphia women that asked the question: "Have you ever slept with Wilt Chamberlain?"

"Do you get the feeling that if the Warren Commission had investigated Wilt Chamberlain's sex life, they would have found only one woman?"
— *Jay Leno*

"Can you imagine living next door to Wilt? The words 'Oh my God' were probably said more than at Saint Mary's Cathedral."
— *Bob Sarlatte*

"Now I know why they call him Wilt."
— a woman reader of Herb Caen's column in the *San Francisco Chronicle*

Mixed Media

For many years, basketball was very nearly a minor sport in the United States, a distant third in popularity behind the big two of football and baseball. But now that James Naismith's game has become a worldwide phenomenon, a wide range of celebrities—Jack Nicholson, Arsenio Hall, Spike Lee, Dyan Cannon, and many more—call themselves basketball fans. What's more, the media's interest has grown by leaps and bounds as well. Here we take a look at some of the people who cover and watch the games from the seats.

Spike Lee, World-Famous Filmmaker, Talks Basketball

On race relations in the NBA: "Why is the 12th guy on every team always white, 6'11" and dorky? Why do you think the Knicks got Kiki [Vandeweghe, a white forward]? Everybody knows Kiki started the demise of the Knicks."

On the Boston Celtics, from the black point of view: "They are the most hated team in the NBA. I'm not talking about the players on the Celtics, but I'm talking about the team, and the image. The players know what they represent and they go harder when they play the Celtics. When the Lakers are playing the Celtics in a championship series, the brothers are praying that Magic or Jabbar is going to pull it out. I'm not going to say all of white America, but a large part of it is saying, 'Come on Celtics, you can't let those niggers beat you.' "

On Larry Bird: "Larry Bird can play, but the way the media has souped him up is unbelievable. The announcer is always going, 'Larry Bird can't jump the highest, but he makes up for it with his blue-collar work ethic.' And blacks are always described as 'gifted' and 'natural.' I think that's unfair to both parties."

On John Thompson and Bobby Knight: "Who do you think gets worse press, Bobby Knight or John Thompson? Bobby Knight is a maniac, throwing this and that, stomping everywhere, but let John Thompson touch a player? Forget about it. He'd be lynched. On national TV no less."

On Patrick Ewing and his newfound popularity in New York: "New York loves him now. But I can remember when these same people were calling him an ape and a baboon and a thug at Georgetown."

Ah Shaddup, Spike!

And now Mike Francesca, a somewhat less famous television commentator, talks about Spike Lee: "Here were three black men, King, Tyson, and Lee, who have risen above any disadvantages they have had. But instead of telling kids, 'Hey, we did it, you can too,' they were essentially saying, 'Forget it. The system won't let it happen.' . . . [Lee is] a big-time sports groupie. He's always high-fiving Patrick Ewing at Knick games. That's what he's into."

Dan Jenkins on Basketball

Dan Jenkins does not write about basketball very much, but when he does, it's usually pretty funny. Some samples:

"Part of the charm of basketball is that it's a simple game to understand. Players race up and down a fairly small area indoors and stuff the ball into a ring with Madonna's dress hanging on it."

"Basketball is no longer for humans. The shortest player on the court can leap over a three-story condominium."

"No sports event compares with the Final Four, not if you want to watch the best scholar athletes do the things they do best. These astounding young men are not only taller than Nepal and capable of slam-dunking a handful of Sherpas, they can quote the great poets and philosophers, solve intricate mathematical problems, and even, in many cases, spell their own names."

"Lord knows, I've tried to watch an NBA game. It was usually one of those games where Michael Jordan scored 62 points and his team lost by 8."

"Why am I so bored trying to watch pro basketball? It probably has something to do with the fact that the season is longer than a Russian winter. Everybody plays half a year and then everybody goes to the playoffs and the games last another three months. When does Jack Nicholson find time to make movies?"

"My own careful study of the sport tells me that the best thing the NBA has going for it is the clock. With only two seconds left in a game, I have personally seen six timeouts called and the lead change hands 12 times."

"There was this game I was watching between a team named for automobile parts and a team named for solar systems. I didn't turn the game on TV until there were only three seconds left because I would still have an hour and a half of basketball to watch."

"Since most basketball games tend to come down to the final few seconds, I have often wondered why all the basketball coaches don't have the life expectancy of goldfish."

Norman Chad, As Well

It isn't just Dan Jenkins who thinks basketball games go on too long. Both Skip Caray ("The last two minutes of some NBA games last longer than some of my marriages") and Norman Chad think they do, too. Chad, a columnist for *Sports Illustrated* and other publications, has written at length about this deplorable trend, particularly in the college ranks:

"The last two minutes of college basketball games have become the Russian breadlines of sport: They never end. Third World nations have been toppled in less time than it takes to play the final moments of some games."

"The game has become a stop-and-start foul-and-be-fouled telethon. The worst offenders are Big East teams. They contest everything; I've seen Big East starters take a charge during player introductions."

"True Big East story: When a Georgetown–Syracuse game began in 1988, there were 15 people watching in my living room. By the time the game was over, the only people left in the room were me and my wife's divorce lawyer."

"New York City closes up earlier than the Big East, for crying out loud. Big East administrators plead to TV execs: 'Please don't put us on at 9 P.M. EST. Not only is it too late for kids, but the only people left at the end are speaking Hawaiian. Big East games take so long that you can actually see the gray creep into the beard of Seton Hall coach P. J. Carlesimo."

"Incidentally, I need to register a mild protest at this point about the Women's Final Four. Don't get me wrong—I'm an ERA guy, a former subscriber to *Ms.*, a big fan of palimony suits—but I turned on CBS just before 5:30 P.M. EST Saturday to catch the *real* Final Four, and instead I got *women* calling timeouts by the bushel. When Sinatra goes on tour, does the opening act run long? Hey, if women want to play some hoop, fine, but not in my living room on my time on semifinal Saturday. . . . I've seen forsythias bloom faster."

And Now, Norman Chad on Dick Vitale

"Now in his 13th season on ESPN and sixth on ABC college basketball telecasts, Vitale is a one-man avalanche of viewer aggravation. College hoops remains the most overanalyzed game on television: There's so much that doesn't need to be said, and Vitale manages to say just about all of it. He is the sport's search and destroy commentator, a fast-break sideshow that often upstages the main event.

"His is a high-pitched, piercing voice with no sense of dimension, an endless shrill of hype and hysteria. He's the car alarm siren that can't be stopped. He's the Lhasa apso barking at your feet. He's the skip in the record that plays over and over. He doesn't observe a game, he obliterates it. He doesn't speak, he shouts. He doesn't soothe, he shatters. Man, he's loud.

"Many claim that Vitale is to college basketball what John Madden is to pro football. But whereas Madden entertains without intruding upon the game, Vitale intrudes without entertaining. Vitale is a huckster. . . . It's a one-note act, played again and again."

What a Few Others Think of Dickie Baby

"The ranting and raving basketball analyst."
—*Howard Cosell*

"Dick Vitale and the Energizer Rabbit, indubitably the two most overexposed creatures on television."
—*Alexander Wolff*, sportswriter

"Teaming Dick Vitale and Jim Valvano to analyze college basketball is akin to staging an Aerosmith concert in a phone booth."
—encore from *Norman Chad*

"Sometimes Dick goes a little too far. When you're on the air for two hours a night, I'd say you should have some journalistic responsibility."
—*Jim Boeheim*, Syracuse coach

"Vitale might be the first sports commentator whose TV monitor comes equipped with an air bag."
—*Steve Kelley*, sportswriter

"Either I left my power drill on or Dick Vitale is back."
—columnist *Brian Schmitz*, noting the beginning of college basketball season

Another Favorite TV Analyst of Ours, Billy Packer

"Billy Packer would analyze a glass of water if allowed."
—*Jake Curtis*, sportswriter

"Billy Packer, from North Carolina, Tobacco Road in the heart of Dixie, may be so provincial that he would have denied landing rights to Columbus."
> —*Howard Cosell*, commenting on Packer's belief that college basketball scholarships should go only to Americans, not foreign-born players

"A throwback to the Chuck Taylor sneaker age."
> —*Gene Wojciechowski*, sportswriter

"As charter members of the Jerry Tarkanian Defense Committee, they [Packer and Dick Vitale] did everything but wear buttons that said FREE THE RUNNIN' REBEL ONE! on television last March. They reworked Tark the Shark's sagging image and turned him loose as Tark the Manatee. Right. We're supposed to believe the NCAA made up all 29 new rules violations it mailed to UNLV president Robert Maxson this spring."
> —*Mike Lupica*, 1991

Other Broadcasters We Have Known

"Ahmad Rashad. He's devoted his broadcasting career to self-promotion and buddying up to the athletes he purports to cover. . . . The man is a case study in the evils of dumping ex-jocks into the broadcast booth."
> —*John Carman*, television critic

"While I'm at it, snide aside to Rashad: We've got the picture—you lift weights with Michael Jordan, you play hoops with him, you hang with him. He probably autographed the Michael Jordan growth-chart poster on your living room wall. You and Air are pals. We believe. Let's move on to other scoops."
> —*Scott Ostler*, columnist

"For slime time it's Pat O'Brien. The late-night anchor is so slick, I can't believe he doesn't slide off his late-night anchor chair. O'Brien is beyond cool; he's cryogenic."
> —*Norman Chad*

"I don't think Mike Francesca has played a game in his life, from the look of his physique. A guy like that shouldn't be talking. I've already had a run-in with Vitale. But at least he knows the game. This guy probably never played a game in his life. I'd like to play him 100 times and shut him out every time."
— former Kansas star *Rex Walters,* on the ex–CBS TV commentator

"Ralph Barbieri picked the Bulls to beat the Lakers in the [1991] NBA finals because 'I don't like anything about the city of Los Angeles.' I pick Bruce McGowan to become the new Sportsphone 68 host on KNBR because I don't like anything about Barbieri."
— *Henry Schulman*, media critic

"Just being around him for a few days makes me all the more sure that when Brown flies, he has to have two seats—one for him, one for his ego."
— columnist *Terry Boers,* on basketball analyst Hubie Brown

"Now over to basketball, where the Dream Team is warming up for its opener against Angola. You'll see the game later, on the regular network, but I'm seeing it live, long before you. And I didn't have to endure the Telestrator analysis of Mike Fratello, who is trying to ruin the English language by saying 'elevate' when he means 'jump.' Mike! Go elevate in a lake."
— *Scott Ostler*

The Brothers Albert

Marv and Steve Albert are the leading brother act in basketball broadcasting. Marv is the broadcaster for the Knicks and NBC's point man in its NBA coverage. "He might be the only guy I know who wears makeup for radio," jokes broadcast mate Mike Fratello. Steve Albert jumped from the New Jersey Nets to Golden State a few years ago, and as such opened himself up to similar good-natured jibes from brother Marv. "Steve will do fine with the Warriors," Marv said after Steve made the move, "as long as they don't get to know him personally." In his own right Steve can claim a Hall of Fame putdown of his former team, a team so miserable that one year their opponents staged promotional giveaways based on how badly they beat the Nets. If the Nets scored under a certain number of points, so the promotion went, the fans who attended the game would get free food. This occurred in a number of NBA cities, culminating in Salt Lake, where the Jazz crushed the Nets, 105–68, and consequently distributed bushels of free food to the locals. Said Steve, "At this rate, the way the Nets are playing, they're going to solve the world hunger problem."

Two Instances in Which Media People Got Dished

The media dishes it out so much, it's always nice when some of it gets thrown back in their faces. A couple of years ago Mike Downey, a columnist for the *Los Angeles Times* who can dish with the best of them, predicted that "Phoenix will fold like a tortilla" prior to the Suns–Lakers playoff series. When, lo and behold, the Suns handled Downey's team in five games, Phoenix fans, at the prompting of KEZ radio in Phoenix, sent him 300 tortillas with the attached note: "We're not sure what you'll do with 300 tortillas. Our listeners have suggested that perhaps you could put them where the sun don't shine."

Down in Dixie, Ailene Voisin, a columnist for the *Atlanta Journal-Constitution,* expressed outrage over a Hawks promotion that featured young, nubile women parading around the Omni in bikinis. Voisin said this was blatantly sexist, and said she wouldn't attend the game. Many sympathized with her protest, others did not. A member of the latter category was club vice president Stan Kasten, who said: "I was crushed Ailene couldn't be there. Tell her I had to put in an extra row of seats for the media that night. We had more reporters than we do for a playoff game."

Book Reviews

Some of our favorite sports books, and the critical comments we've heard about them:

Outrageous! by Charles Barkley and Roy Johnson

"We have come to the point in these life and times sports memoirs where the least believable words are those on the title page after 'by.' Shortly before *Outrageous!* was released, Charles Barkley, listed as its principal author, announced that the book—*his* book allegedly misquoted him, not a lot, mind you, but just in those sections where he criticized his teammates. Outrageous, indeed! If Barkley didn't write this book—and he didn't, of course—doesn't the fan who plunks down $20 for the privilege of reading it have the right to know the exact nature of his participation? . . . Did he, in fact, even bother to read the whole thing before publication, and if not, why not?"

  —*Steve Gietschier*, columnist

  "Its chief fault is the covers are too far apart."

  —*Pat Williams*, Orlando Magic president

Calling the Shots, by Earl Strom with Blaine Johnson

"A referee writing a book makes about as much sense as players' wives signing autographs."

  —*Dave Cowens*, former NBA star

Full Court Pressure, by Kentucky coach Rick Pitino

"The overriding sense of this book is that Pitino came to poor ol' good-for-nothin' Kentucky and by the power of his talent turned lead into gold."

  —*Dave Kindred*, sports columnist

MBA: Management By Auerbach, by Red Auerbach

"No highfalutin language, promises Chrysler's Lee Iacocca in his foreword. In fact, it's barely lowfalutin. . . . Auerbach's catechism is delivered under the rubric 'Red Sez.' Now, Red Sez may be almost as catchy as Bo Knows. The problem is that Bo and everybody else with any common sense already knows everything Red Sez. What borders on the offensive is the sneaking suspicion that Red doesn't even believe every trite thing he sez. Just three pages after he preaches how essential it is to embrace change, he vows

that the Celtics will never feature popular NBA 'gimmickry' such as cheerleaders and mascots 'as long as I'm around.' "
—*Mark Starr*, book reviewer

The Selling of the Green, a critical look at Red Auerbach's Boston Celtics

"I didn't read it. I won't read it. People have told me about parts of it. I don't even want to talk about what those guys said about us. It's just an extreme way to sell a book, like a supermarket tabloid. We don't look at the skin. I don't care if we have 10 blacks or 10 whites. If that's what it takes to win, then that's what we're going to do."
—*Red Auerbach*

Taking to the Air, a biography of Michael Jordan, by Jim Naughton

"It's another microwave jock bio with about as much literary value as a satin starter jacket."
—*Peter Plagens*, book reviewer

Hang Time: Days and Dreams with Michael Jordan, by Bob Greene

"Chicago columnist Bob Greene is writing a book about his pal, Michael Jordan. Diabetics, beware."
—*John Hillyer*, sportswriter

Rotisserie League Basketball

Rotisserie basketball is an offshoot of the baseball version of the game. The book *Rotisserie League Basketball,* edited by Greg Kelly, is a guide for people who want to play the game and includes some of the funniest sportswriting being done anywhere. Its assessments of NBA players—published without attribution, but one suspects that *Sports Illustrated* writers and rotisserie players Steve Wulf, Steve Rushin, and Jack McCallum had something to do with them—are hilarious. There are outrageously bad puns, song parodies, large heapings of sarcasm and ridicule, anagrams (Tyrone Bogues: "one bogus trey"), plays on words, and jokes aplenty. Herewith a sampling of the high (and low) wit of *Rotisserie League Basketball:*

Gerald Wilkins: "Upon kissing the tarmac on U.S. soil, American POWs told harrowing tales of how their Iraqi captors, in violation of the Geneva convention, forced them to watch films of Wilkins leading the Knick fast break."

Rex Chapman: "Leaps like a brother, shoots like your mother."

Mike Gminski: "Alas for Gminski, the ball rarely goes inski."

Joe Kleine: "A rabid fan of 'The Andy Griffith Show,' he looks like Otis, rebounds like Aunt Bee, spends more time sitting on his butt than Floyd the Barber, and like Barney, is not allowed to shoot."

Dan Schayes: "The good news—he has finally begun to play like Dolph. The bad news—Dolph is 63 years old."

The oft-injured Michael Adams: "The Michael Adams doll—pull his string, he pulls his hamstrings."

Lance Blanks: "With the possible exception of Rolando Blackman, there's probably not a more aptly named player in the NBA. Check out his shooting percentage."

Jon Koncak: "Never one to run his mouth or feign injury, Koncak simply goes out and gets you 4 points and 4 rebounds every single night."

A. J. English: "English need only look to his first name to figure out what he needs: A J."

Byron Scott: "Like the absorbent paper towel for which he's named, this Scott is starting to suck."

Joe Wolf: "Last year we told you that Wolf, a native of Kohler, Wisconsin, the Urinal Capital of the World, had trouble spraying his shots. This year, we regret to inform you that dribbling is also a problem for Joe."

The Basketball Roast

"**I**f you don't play ball," said Dean Meminger, "you can't hang out." Here are some one-liners, gags, insults, jokes, and other stuff intended to entertain and amuse while you're hanging out waiting for the next game.

Stanley Roberts Fat Jokes, by Pat Williams

Stanley Roberts is as big as Manute Bol is thin. He stands seven feet tall and weighs over 300 pounds, and when he was picked by the Orlando Magic in the 1991 draft, Pat Williams, the Magic's president, had a field day making jokes about him. Roberts is no longer with the Magic, but Williams's jokes can still draw a laugh.

"Stanley thinks a balanced meal is a Big Mac in each hand."

"We got him started eating the seven basic food groups, and now there are only three left."

"There's a thin man inside of Stanley—he's ordering a hot fudge sundae."

"Stanley's Florida driver's license says, 'Photo continued on other side.'"

"Stanley attended the Macy's Thanksgiving Day parade—wearing ropes."

"Whoever said no man is an island never saw Stanley in a swimming pool."

"Stanley's chosen his burial site—Montana."

"We told Stanley to go on a water diet, and Lake Superior disappeared."

"Stanley says his two favorite things are eating and watching TV. So we decided to combine the two, and now he's eating out of his satellite dish."

"We have Stanley into heavy lifting, so now he takes his lunch to work."

"His idea of a salad is putting a piece of lettuce on top of a pizza."

Stanley Roberts Thin Jokes, by Pat Williams

As you might expect, Stanley got annoyed with all these jokes about his heft. When he signed with the Magic he asked his new boss to cease and desist. Williams agreed, and promptly started making thin jokes about Stanley:

"He's so thin now his pajamas have only one stripe."

"He can't go to the movies because his seat won't stay down."

"Stanley's diet has created havoc. McDonald's and Wendy's have sued him for nonsupport. But I must say that even when Stanley came in, he carried his weight well. It just took two trips. But all of that is in the past. I can't use those jokes anymore. Stanley has turned over a new chin."

Other Stanley Roberts Jokes

"Someone better draft this player before he explodes."
—columnist *Mark Heisler*, after Roberts's weight ballooned from 290 to 310 pounds in a two-week period before the 1991 draft

"I think if Stanley went swimming, somebody would harpoon him."
—*Marty Blake*, NBA scout

"Stanley Roberts' eating habits might be getting out of hand. After a recent game, he tried to order from the turnover column on the stat sheet."
—*Peter Vecsey*, USA *Today*

"Stanley's lost 20 pounds, so that means he doesn't have to travel by barge anymore."
—columnist *Larry Guest*, after Stanley went on a diet and dropped to a svelte 299

"With Stanley Roberts and John Williams anchoring the [Los Angeles] roster, the Clippers are over the calorie cap."
—*Shaun Powell*, sportswriter, after Roberts moved over to the Clippers

One very meaty guy (Stanley Roberts) gets penned between another meaty guy (Kevin Duckworth) and Jerome Kersey. (Photo by Joe Gosen)

More Pro Wide Bodies

"Two people could give him a massage and never meet one another."
> —columnist *Mitch Albom*, on center Kevin Duckworth (described by another sportswriter as a "seven-foot, 290-pound tower of jello")

"It's tough getting through there. They probably could have the All-Butt team all by themselves."
> —forward *Xavier McDaniel*, on trying to drive to the basket against Rick Mahorn and Charles Barkley

"All that Mills has ever proven is that he can run a cheeseburger down his throat in 4.5 seconds."
> —sportswriter *Jackie MacMullan*, on forward Terry Mills

"If Benoit hadn't eaten in two days and he was thrown into a cage with a grizzly bear, you can rest assured somebody would come out wearing a fur coat."
> —*Cedric Maxwell*, on the big-eating, 300-pound Benoit Benjamin

"He's so fat that his bathtub has stretch marks."
> —*Pat Williams*, on the young and tubby Charles Barkley

More Pat Williams Lines on Many Other Things

Who writes this guy's material? Besides all his Stanley Roberts jokes, the presiding wit of the Orlando Magic has lots of other great one-liners, such as:

On Manute Bol: "He looks like he went to the bloodbank and forgot to say 'when.'"

On agents: "What do you have when you've got an agent buried up to his neck in sand? Answer: not enough sand."

After David Stern signed a five-year, $27.5 million contract in 1990 to continue as NBA commissioner: "All I know is that on airplane trips David's wallet will be considered carry-on baggage."

"In David Stern's neighborhood, the Salvation Army band has a string section, and the bird feeders have salad bars."

"David is about to move into a neighborhood where the Girl Scouts go door to door selling croissants. And every spring, kids sign up for Little League polo."

"One of David's sons asked him if he could buy a chemistry set, so David went out and bought the DuPont Company."

On the salesmanship qualities of David Stern: "We have had people in this league who would have had trouble selling Blue Cross to Humpty Dumpty. David Stern could sell an anvil to a drowning man. He can sell a pogo stick to a kangaroo. David Stern could sell a stethoscope to a tree surgeon. He won't be happy until he walks the streets of Peking and sees every kid wearing an NBA hat."

On Gary Bettman, after the former NBA executive was named commissioner of the National Hockey League: "I gave Gary a hockey puck once, and he spent the rest of the day trying to open it."

On the Magic's losing record: "We can't win at home. We can't win on the road. As general manager, I just can't figure out where else to play."

After the Miami Heat lost 17 straight games at the start of their first-ever season: "The Heat lose so much, their mascot should be a Democrat."

Frank Layden Lines

Frank Layden, the rotund former coach, now president of the Utah Jazz, is another front-office administrator with a sharp wit. Some samples:

On newspaper reporter Peter Vecsey: "Peter Vecsey is to journalism what Dr. Ruth is to medicine."

On his beefy size: "I don't know, but I stepped on a scale that gives fortune cards, and the card read, 'Come back in 15 minutes—alone.' "

After diminutive Charlotte owner George Shinn criticized him as a sloppy dresser: "It's easy to dress a midget. And who sets the styles? Charlotte? They all wear loafers down there. They don't even know how to tie their shoes."

On coach Doug Moe's waterbed: "I understand Doug gave his wife a waterbed for Christmas, but she calls it the Dead Sea."

On the big-bucks contract of NBA commissioner David Stern: "The head of the Columbian cartel doesn't make that much money."

On seeing Morganna, the "kissing bandit," appear at a Utah Jazz game: "When I saw her coming I hollered for the police. I thought someone stole the ball bag."

Good Lines on Bad Shooters (Pros)

Legend has it that when he was growing up in his native Sudan, Manute Bol killed a lion with a spear. After seeing Manute shoot a basketball in the NBA, Peter Vecsey remarked: "Now I'm certain that he killed that lion with a free throw." Jeff Weinstock said that Manute has "that sky throw that starts down in Louisiana and is released up near Greenland. It usually lands about there too." Some more bad shooters from the pro ranks:

"If this were football, every time Anthony and Jackson shoot, they'd be accused of intentional grounding."

> —another jab from *Peter Vecsey*, this time about Knick guards Greg Anthony and Mark Jackson

"He has never taken a shot that he couldn't miss."

> —sportswriter *Paul Ladewski*, on guard Gerald Wilkins

"You could lock him in a gym for an hour by himself and he couldn't score 20 points."

> —Knicks executive *Al Bianchi*, on Dennis Rodman

"The thing is, Houston's guards don't have a clue. Vernon Maxwell . . . wouldn't know a good shot from a horrendous heave if you hit him with a polo mallet."

> —*Tom Kertes*, sportswriter

"The next time the New Jersey Nets' Chris Dudley is fouled, he should decline the penalty."

> —columnist *Allan Malamud*, on the man who set an NBA record (1 for 18) for foul-shooting ineptitude

"Orlando hosts the Ice Follies every time Jerry Reynolds throws up a shot."
> —*Rotisserie League Basketball*

"He [Scott Roth] broke his nose for the ninth time last season. Alas, his shot is no straighter than his septum."
> —more from *Rotisserie League Basketball*

Bad Shooters (College)

"After watching LSU center Shaquille O'Neal shoot free throws Saturday night against Duke, I can understand why some people are calling him the next Wilt Chamberlain."
> —*Allan Malamud*

"UNLV's Moses Scurry . . . ran over to Ball State's bench after the Rebels survived a 69–67 squeaker and pretended to fire his fingers like six guns at the players. Ball State coach Dick Hunsaker was furious, although he had nothing to fear from Scurry. If his box score was any indication —one shot, no points, no rebounds— Scurry couldn't have touched them if he'd been shooting real pistols."
> —*C. W. Nevius*, at the 1990 tournament game between UNLV and Ball State

Bad Shooters (Celebrity Division)

"It's a success when he hits the backboard when he shoots."
> —*Ahmad Rashad*, on actor Bruce Boxleitner competing in a celebrity basketball special (Al McGuire added: "Hell, it's a success if he hits the floor when he dribbles")

Good Lines About Bad Defensive Players (Pros)

"He is a graduate of the Blue Bayou School of Defense: 'Hey Winston, that guy just blew by you.' "
> —basketball analyst *Bob Bellotti*, on Winston Garland

"What is it about Charles Jones of Washington that keeps him in the league? His defense stinks. He ought to have a road sign that says THIS LANE OPEN tacked to his jersey."
> —*Bob Bellotti*

"Mullin likes to call rookie teammate Mitch Richmond 'Rock' because that's how solid the first-year man was all season. But not on defense, where Richmond was as pliable as a fat man's belly."
> —*Bob Bellotti*

"And what about Reggie Theus? He doesn't really guard people at all, does he? Why is he called a guard? Shouldn't there be another name for him?"
> —*Rotisserie League Basketball*

Bad Defensive Players (College)

"They tell me you can't guard a telephone pole."
> —coach *Don Haskins*, assessing one of his recruits at the University of Texas at El Paso

One Good Line About a Bad Rebounder (College)

"Dead people could get rebounds if they're out there 50 minutes."
> —Syracuse coach *Jim Boeheim*, commenting after one of his players failed to get a defensive rebound in two games

Good Lines About Bad Teams (Pro)

"We put it all together. Unfortunately, everything was bad."
> —*Jimmy Rodgers*, Minnesota Timberwolves coach, after a loss

"We're going to be exciting. Of course, it was exciting when the *Titanic* went down."
> —coach *Bob Weiss*, sizing up his Atlanta Hawks before a season

"Evander Holyfield would have been the perfect owner for the Houston Rockets. He'll never beat anyone of significance, and neither will they."
>—*Michael Ventre*, sportswriter

"The other day, I was walking down the street and three guys jumped out of a car and forced me to take a Timberwolves jacket and cap from them."
>—*Gerry Heroff*, Minnesota comic, on his home team

"I was driving on the highway in New Jersey and saw a sign. It said INTERSTATE 95, NETS 91."
>—*John Salley*, basketball player and comedian

"If the Denver Nuggets start chartering flights for road games, the plane should be named Air Farce One."
>—*Woody Paige*, sports columnist

"A week ago, when George Karl came in from Spain to coach Seattle, he forgot himself and spoke in Spanish to his players during his first game. Spanish. English. These guys have trouble understanding basketball in any language."
>—*Jack McCallum*, on the Seattle SuperSonics after
>George Karl was hired as coach in early 1992

"People say, 'How could you blow a 10- to 15-point lead?' I say: 'Pretty easy.' The question is: How did we get one in the first place?"
>—*Jerry Reynolds*, then coaching the Sacramento Kings

Good Lines About Bad Teams (College)

"Arizona's biggest problem is that the Iditarod ended two weeks ago. Susan Butcher's the only person who could have whipped them to the Final Four."
>—as told to sportswriter Alexander Wolff, after Arizona lost badly to East Tennessee State in the 1992 NCAAs

"UCLA has two problems: neurological and cardiovascular. No brains, no heart."
—remark about recent Bruin team

"Things got so bad that I had to play my student manager for a while. They got really bad when she started to complain to the press that she wasn't getting enough playing time."
—*Linda Hil-McDonald*, Minnesota women's basketball coach, on a losing team one year

Dogs

"Duckworth has enormous talent, but he's not using it. He's on my all Ken-L-Ration team."
—Eastern Conference coach, on the center for the Portland Trail Blazers (a team that, in reference to Duckworth, was once called "four greyhounds and a basset hound")

"All Star? Sidney Wicks an All Star? The only team you could make is the All Dog Team."
—*Jack McCloskey*, then head coach of the expansion Portland Trail Blazers, in a conversation with Wicks when he was a rookie in the early 1970s

"[Joe Barry Carroll is] the real Mailman: He's slow, doesn't deliver and is surrounded by dogs."
—*Rotisserie League Basketball,* on Carroll with the Denver Nuggets

"I think George Karl will be an excellent coach for the Sonics—if there is an excellent coach for the Sonics. If you sleep with dogs, you get a lot of fleas, and those people in Seattle are sleeping with a lot of fleas."
—NBA coach, as told to *Tacoma News Tribune,* after Karl was hired as Sonics coach in 1992

Thou Shalt Not Pass

"There is no truth to the rumor that Smith had kidney stones last season, and still didn't want to pass."
>—*Rotisserie League Basketball,* on Clippers forward Charles Smith

"Our motto is 'This, too, shall pass,' although some of our players won't."
>—*Pat Williams*, on a spate of injuries that forced the Magic to try a number of different lineups one season

"That's the one with all the No Passing signs."
>—deejay *Tom Hughes*, speculating on what a Dominique Wilkins Highway would be like

"If 'Nique were in a phone booth with Mark Eaton, he would think he was open."
>—Hawks coach *BobWeiss,* on Dominique Wilkins

"For a team that would rather pass a stone than the ball, it's amazing the way they've been playing."
>—comment a few years ago about the Atlanta Hawks of Wilkins, Doc Rivers, Moses Malone, etc.

Dim Bulbs (Pro)

"You know there are times that he can be a really interesting, pleasant conversationalist, and the next time you talk to him, you look over at him and suddenly realize nobody's home."
>—anonymous Milwaukee Buck player, on teammate Dale Ellis

"I tried to pick his mind. It took me three minutes."
>—*Larry Bird*, jesting about fellow Dream Teamer Patrick Ewing (who replied, "It took me one for you")

Dominique Wilkins in a typical pose: not passing the ball. (Photo courtesy of the Atlanta Hawks)

"He's a quick learner, but he forgets quick too."
>—*Mychal Thompson*, on Lakers teammate Vlade Divac

Dim Bulbs (College)

"If his IQ was any lower, we'd have to water him."
>—*Rick Dees*, then coaching Wyoming, on one of his recruits

"Nine out of 10 UCLA students have absolutely no idea where in the world Duke University is located or whether it was endowed by John Wayne or named after Patty."
>—*Mike Downey*, Los Angeles columnist

Geezers (Pro and College)

"He is the only guy who goes one on one with an oxygen tank on his back."
>—*Larry Bird*, after playing a pickup game with aging Celtic boss Red Auerbach

"I've been here so long that when I got here, the Dead Sea wasn't even sick."
>—*Wimp Sanderson*, longtime Alabama basketball coach (since retired)

Bad Haircuts

"It looks like a bobcat is perched on his head."
>—*George Shirk*, on the hairdo of Warriors forward Tom Tolbert

"A mushroom gone wildly to seed."
>—another comment on Tolbert's hairstyle

"This is how they wear it in Southern California. Maybe in five years, they'll catch up in Northern California and everybody will wear it like this."
>—*Tom Tolbert*, responding to his critics in the Bay Area
[Editor's note: It's doubtful, Tom.]

"In case you missed the episode of 'Unsolved Mysteries' that was devoted to the subject, scientists now believe that Walker's head is not sporting a hairdo at all; instead, they theorize, the Walkman is wearing a bishop's mitre, made from human hair."
>—*Rotisserie League Basketball,* on Kenny Walker's do

"He is the most unlikely superstar in the league. If you didn't know him and he was standing against the fence at the playground, you might take him last. 'All right, who gets Bristlehead?' "
>—*Rick Reilly*, in an offhand jibe at Chris Mullin's crew
cut, described by another writer as a "retro Bazooka
Joe look"

Benchwarmers

Benchwarmers are the forgotten men of basketball. Forgotten, that is, by all but their own family. "Daddy," said little Nicholas Rollins to his father, Tree Rollins, who was sitting at the end of the Atlanta Hawks bench during a game, "if you're not going to play in the game, why can't you sit in the stands with us?"

Sorry, no, the reserves can't do that because if they did, who would be there to hold down the end of the bench? Who would slap high fives with one another and wave their towels around when their team did something great on the floor? Who would clear out of their chairs and huddle around the starters during a time-out? And how could you ever do a proper layup drill without the reserves? And who'd be around to come in at the end of the game during garbage time?

Benchwarmers have a very important job, as Scott Hastings and Ed Nealy will testify. During the summer they staged—well, they talked about staging, at any rate—their own basketball camp, teaching young kids how to warm the bench just like they did in the pros. Here's Scott, on the benefits of such a training camp:

"Ed and I have much in common, primarily spending time on the bench, so we put our experience into our camp instruction. Instead of fast-break drills, we run the slow-break drill. That's when five guys fight to see who's the last person down the court. Other drills include the flat-footed jumper, the screen-and-screen-and-screen-some-more drill, the floor-burn hip pointer drill, the stand-on-a-chair dunking drill, the bag-carrying drill, and of course, our favorite, the how-to-move-your-family-in-24-hours drill."

Basketball versus Baseball

The differences between basketball and baseball? Steve Wulf has a whole host of them, namely:

"Larry Bird and Doug Bird.

"Basketball players do it in their underwear; baseball players do it in their pajamas.

"Basketball players are athletic. (Cecil Fielder has as much body fat as the entire NBA.)

"Bill Russell and Bill Russell.

"Baseball has 300-pound umpires with the mind-set of teamsters. Basketball has physically fit referees who realize the players are bigger than they are.

"Basketball has Sleepy (Floyd), Happy (Hairston), and Doc (Rivers). Baseball has Grumpy (Barry Bonds) and Dopey (Jose Canseco).

"In basketball, turnovers are a statistical category. In baseball, turnovers are part of the pregame spread . . ."

So those are Steve's opinions. His colleague Greg Kelly offers another: "We [basketball fans] worship the air Michael Jordan walks on, and our patron saint is Jack Nicholson. Baseball's is George Will, which tells you everything you need to know about baseball, doesn't it?"

For the final opinion on the subject, we turn to Bill Russell—the *basketball* Bill Russell—who once had a teammate on the Celtics named Gene Conley. Conley was a kind of fifties version of Bo Jackson or Deion Sanders, a guy good enough to play two professional sports. In Conley's case, the sports were basketball, which wore him out, and baseball. As Russell explains, "He told me he couldn't wait for the basketball season to end, so he could go back to baseball and get out of shape."

Smart Alecks

After Arkansas coach Nolan Richardson said about Anfernee Hardaway, "If you took Larry Bird, Magic Johnson, and Michael Jordan, and rolled them all together, that's the way I see Hardaway," Tony Kornheiser cracked, "Nolan, here's cab fare. Go to an ophthalmologist."

After the Miami Heat blew a big lead, their disgusted center, John Salley, remarked, "We played like a bunch of college girls." To which an unidentified Boston Celtic responded: "I guess John hasn't been watching TV lately. He's not half as good as some of those college girls."

After hearing former basketball great and now United States Senator Bill Bradley speak, Dave Barry commented that "Bradley has all the charisma of gravel."

In 1987, while he was playing for Alabama, Derrick McKey was leaving the floor after the Crimson Tide had smashed Vanderbilt in a game. "That's all right," hollered a Vanderbilt rooter. "In 10 years you'll be working for me." McKey, who's now in the pros, replied, "Not unless you buy the Knicks."

After Quinn Buckner compared himself to Magic Johnson, his broadcast mate Bob Costas said, "If you're going to put yourself in the same breath with Magic, then I'm going to start comparing myself to Edward R. Murrow."

After beefy center Oliver Miller criticized Charles Barkley for setting a "bad example" on the court, Barkley said to him, "You can't even jump high enough to touch the rim, unless they put a Big Mac on it."

After Charles Barkley said that he wouldn't mind playing NFL football after retiring from basketball, teammate Rick Mahorn told him, "With that head of yours, all you'll need is a chin strap."

After a fan yelled at Charles Barkley, "You're never going to get a championship ring—never!" Sir Charles turned to him and said, "That's okay. I have $20 million, so I can afford to buy one."

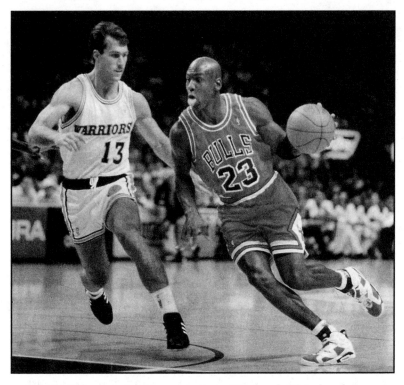

Don't stick your tongue out at us, Michael. This book is over.
(Photo by Brad Mangin)

Index

(Page numbers in italics refer to photographs.)

About the Author

Kevin Nelson has published books on baseball and football insults, as well as several other sports books. He is always interested in hearing the latest insults in basketball or any other sport. If you've heard any good ones lately, you can write him at P.O. Box 1221, Benicia, CA 94510.